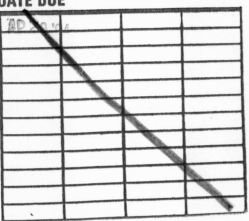

THE
REFERENCE
SHELF

THE STATE OF U.S. EDUCATION

edited by ROBERT EMMET LONG

THE REFERENCE SHELF

Volume 63 Number 5

THE H. W. WILSON COMPANY

New York   1991

THE REFERENCE SHELF

The books in this series contain reprints of articles, excerpts from books, and addresses on current issues and social trends in the United States and other countries. There are six separately bound numbers in each volume, all of which are generally published in the same calendar year. One number is a collection of recent speeches; each of the others is devoted to a single subject and gives background information and discussion from various points of view, concluding with a comprehensive bibliography that contains books and pamphlets and abstracts of additional articles on the subject. Books in the series may be purchased individually or on subscription.

Library of Congress Cataloging-in-Publication Data

Main entry under title:

The State of U.S. education / edited by Robert Emmet Long.
    p.   cm. — (The Reference shelf ; v. 63, no. 5)
    Compilation of articles.
    Includes bibliographical references.

    ISBN 0-8242-0816-1
    1. Educational change—United States.   2. Minorities—Education-United States—Curricula.   3. School, Choice of—United States.
4. Education, Urban—United States.   I. Long, Robert Emmet.
II. Series.
  LA217.2.S73   1991
  370´.973—dc20   91-20484
                                            CIP

Cover: Eager elementary school students getting off the bus.
Photo: The Image Works

Printed in the United States of America

CONTENTS

PREFACE

The state of the American public schools was a subject of controversy throughout the 1980s, a debate highlighted by the report "A Nation at Risk," issued in 1983 by the U.S. Department of Education's National Commission on Excellence in Education. The report, which called for sweeping education reform, was the centerpiece of the Reference Shelf title *American Education* (Volume 56, Number 5), which I edited in 1984. Since then other developments have occurred in the field of secondary education, and it now seems appropriate to survey the situation of the schools in this new, updated volume. What this collection makes clear is that although improvements have been made, such as the introduction of merit pay for superior teachers and an upgrading of teachers' salaries in a number of cases, the country's school districts are still performing inadequately. Despite a series of reform movements in the 1980s and '90s, the problems affecting the schools have proved difficult to overcome; panaceas are no longer expected but a prevailing interest in experimentation may yet lead to a higher standard of performance in the nation's schools.

Section One of this volume presents strong evidence that the public schools continue to falter—as evidenced by the poor showing of American students as measured by international test scores, and by the failure of many high school students to meet basic standards of literacy and computation. Nor is there any consensus as to who is at fault or what is to be done. Two articles in this section are critical of the educational establishment and call for greater teacher-administration accountability, while other articles fault the Bush administration's lack of leadership. Concluding selections point out some of the initiatives that the states are now carrying out, and the latest announcement of a new education reform policy from the Bush White House.

Section Two deals with innovations in curriculum, particularly the new emphasis on multiculturalism designed to keep step with the interests and needs of the increasing number of school children of minority group background. The articles in this section center upon "A Curriculum of Inclusion," a 1989 report to the New York State Commissioner of Education by the Task Force on Minorities that calls for a vastly enlarged role of minority cultures in teaching materials authorized by the state. The pieces that follow it are sharply critical of the report and its notion of pluralism, claiming that this approach, rather than promoting a blending of cultures within the dominant one would achieve a greater separateness of minority cultures.

Section Three examines issues of financing and choice in the restructuring of schools. Particular attention is given to the new option of choice in parents' selection of a school for their children. Choice is already in effect in many school districts throughout the nation but the concept seems likely to be expanded, through a system of tuition credits, so that students may also choose to attend a private school. Others advocate the inclusion of parochial schools as well, even though the constitution expressly provides for a separation of church and state. But however the choice concept develops, it will have far-reaching implications for public education as it now exists.

Finally, Section Four examines the state of inner-city schools in large urban areas, which are regarded by many as breeding grounds of academic and personal failure. However, the situation of the inner-city schools, while bleak, may not be beyond repair, as some of the articles maintain.

The editor is indebted to the authors and publishers who have granted permission to reprint the materials in this compilation. Special thanks are due to Joyce Cook and the Fulton (N.Y.) Public Library staff, to Fulton's G. Ray Bodley school library, and to the staff of Penfield Library, State University of New York at Oswego.

ROBERT EMMET LONG

April 1991

I. EDUCATION REFORM: THE SITUATION AT PRESENT

EDITOR'S INTRODUCTION

The opening section of this compilation considers the situation of the public schools in the late 1980s and early 1990s, in the aftermath of "A Nation at Risk," with its urgent call for education reform. The "excellence movement" attracted widespread attention in the 1980s, but performance in the schools remains disappointing, as Elizabeth Ehrlich concludes in the opening article, reprinted from *Business Week*. Top-ranked students compare well with their peers in industrialized countries abroad, but many others have failed to master even basic skills. A million young people drop out of our high schools every year, and of those who graduate as many as 25 percent cannot read or write at the eighth grade level.

In the following article, Carl F. Kaestle, writing for *American Heritage* magazine provides a historical overview of public education reform in the United States. "Schools always have had plenty of critics," he observes, "but widespread reform has succeeded only when there has been a general crisis of confidence in the schools and reformers have solidified public consensus about what changes are needed." The third selection, written by Janet Raloff and reprinted from *Science News*, discusses two recent studies conducted by the National Science Foundation, one of which reveals that compared to students' math and science achievement in 17 countries tested, U.S. students ranked from fair to poor. The second study indicates worrisome problems in the teaching of math and science in the U.S., where more time is given to lecturing than to hands-on projects, and where courses in chemistry and physics are often taught by teachers who studied some other field.

In a strongly worded article in *Fortune*, Myron Magnet stresses the failure of basic knowledge of history and literature among students today. Magnet attributes this inadequacy to progressive education, which has resulted in the dilution of content in textbooks, the substitution of electives such as "bachelor living" for more substantive courses, and the near elimination of homework requirements. Reform movements in a number of states, including New Jersey, he points out, are now emphasizing greater teacher accountability and more stringent tests for high school graduation—and in some cases, for promotion from grade to grade. In a related article, appearing in *Commentary*, Chester E. Finn, Jr., notes the conflict in education reform between those who would impose greater standardization and those who urge greater "empowerment" of local teachers and principals. Finn argues that "civilian" control, as opposed to control by educators, is essential if content is to be restored to education, since the "process method" favored by teachers works against their pupils' acquiring specific knowledge.

Written before the appointment of Lamar Alexander as Secretary of Education, an article by Ann Reilly Dowd in *Fortune* begins by noting the discrepancy between President Bush's education rhetoric and his failure to mount a concerted effort to improve the country's schools. Dowd sees the burden of improving education falling largely now on the states and describes the steps that a number of them are taking.

AMERICA'S SCHOOLS
STILL AREN'T MAKING THE GRADE[1]

Americans have always asked a lot of their schools: Civilize the frontier with the three Rs, assimilate immigrants, secure U.S. military might by bolstering high school science. At its most fundamental, democracy aspires to produce literate, responsible citizens. But social and economic change has continually reshaped what school is expected to do—from training homemakers to fostering integration.

A new call for school reform is ringing across the land. This one is different: The nation's economic problems are being placed at the schoolhouse door. Economic growth, competitive-

[1]Article by Elizabeth Ehrlich. Reprinted from the Sept. 19, 1988 issue of *Business Week*, by special permission, copyright © 1991 by McGraw-Hill, Inc.

ness, and living standards depend heavily on making investments in human capital. That means attending to the state of America's schools.

It is a worrisome state. Although top-ranked U.S. students compare well with their peers in industrialized nations, the rest do worse. One million young people drop out of high school every year. Rates approach 50% in some inner cities. Of the 2.4 million who graduate, as many as 25% cannot read or write at the eighth-grade, or "functionally literate," level, according to some estimates. Most 17-year-olds in school cannot summarize a newspaper article, write a good letter requesting a job, solve real-life math problems, or follow a bus schedule.

What's needed is a do-or-die battle to turn the schools around. But the front lines are weary—and fresh recruits are scarce. Between retirement and normal attrition, America could need to replace 1 million teachers—half the current force—before the end of the century. But only 8% of today's 1.6 million college freshmen say they're interested in teaching, and half of those will typically change their minds. Worse, half of all new hires leave teaching within seven years. And with shortages of educated workers looming throughout the economy, schools will be competing with other sectors for quality candidates.

The demand for school reform has been percolating since the mid-1970s, when declining results on standardized tests raised concerns about basic skills. It exploded in 1983, after the National Commission on Excellence in Education released *A Nation at Risk*. Warning of a "rising tide of mediocrity" in public schools, it called for rigorous academic standards and a standardized, traditional high school curriculum of history, Western literature, foreign languages, science, and math.

Critics still blast the report as elitist or oversimplified. But few deny that our schools need fixing. "If a company was turning out 90% lemons, we would rethink the whole production process," says Albert Shanker, president of the American Federation of Teachers (AFT). "This is not a question of a few recalls. The system is producing lemons."

Most Americans want to do something about it. In a 1987 Harris Poll, 90% of those surveyed endorsed the principle that "for the U.S. to become competitive, we must pay more for quality education" and get "tangible results."

The tricky question: how to get those results. Educators are sharply divided. Some endorse the call for strengthening the traditional curriculum. AFT's Shanker would give teachers a freer hand to restructure the classroom environment. Others say schools must take on new family-like roles to nurture the growing numbers of poor or troubled kids in the system.

Predictably, conservatives deride the idea that schools should depart from traditional teaching formulas to suit individual learning styles or to respond to students' social problems. They stress the importance of expectation and high standards, holding up such examples as William Lloyd Garrison School, where South Bronx kids from low-income families test at or above grade levels in reading. "You don't change the principles of medicine when patients have poorer health or a poorer state of nutrition," insists outgoing Education Secretary William J. Bennett. When Bennett urges school overhaul, he means a shift of power from the educational Establishment—teachers' unions, administrators, and colleges of education—to parents, citizens, and state legislatures.

Traditionalists point to Japan, where students seem to perform as well as or better at all levels than U.S. kids. Japanese mothers are highly involved in their children's schooling, teachers are respected and well-paid, the school year is longer, and more homework is given. "The Japanese system," says Bennett, "is pretty close to a system of education that is universal and of quality."

Those for whom tradition is not a panacea say American schools must change with the times. They argue that the public school system was organized along factory lines in the 1920s by a society enchanted by mass production. Classrooms were standardized, and decisions about teaching methods and content were passed from state offices to superintendents to principals and finally to the chalk-wielding line workers: teachers. After a 50-minute class, the bell rang and pupils moved on. "If the student is viewed as an inanimate object moving on an assembly line, this makes perfect sense," Shanker says.

Successful companies, as Xerox Corp. Chairman David T. Kearns [appointed Under Secretary of Education in March 1991] notes in *Winning the Brain Race*, "have discarded the archaic, outmoded, and thoroughly discredited practices that are still in place in most of our large school districts: top-down, command-control management—a system designed to stifle creativity and independent judgment."

To education reformers, it is significant that the Japanese themselves are beginning to worry that their nation's learning style, heavily based on rote and memorization, doesn't promote creative thinking and flexible skills. "In Japan they do harder and longer what we do, and get better results," argues Adam Urbanski, president of the Rochester (N.Y.) Teachers Assn. "The purpose of reform is to do it differently—to challenge the fundamental structure."

Indeed, concerns about basic skills already have produced some improvements along traditional lines. Educational Testing Service (ETS), a testing-and-research organization based in Princeton, N.J., reports that test scores in math, reading, computer literacy, and science have gone up since the mid-1970s. Most of that came from minority kids, who increased from 16% to 23% of all schoolchildren. But "the bad news is that we haven't budged in improving higher-order skills, critical-thinking skills," says Archie E. LaPointe, head of ETS's National Assessment of Educational Progress (NAEP).

It's higher order skills that a sophisticated economy increasingly needs. "Over the long term, basic skills only give you the right to compete against the Third World for Third World wages," notes Marc S. Tucker, chairman of the National Center on Education & the Economy in Rochester, N.Y. To achieve more advanced goals, "I'd like to see a lot less of kids sitting quietly in rows and a lot more deeply engaged in projects in which they are heavily invested, which require them to learn a lot."

Tucker maintains that most kids don't learn well by listening to a lecture or reading the text. He and others advocate peer tutoring, team learning, simulation games, and other nontraditional approaches, particularly for disadvantaged children for whom formal classrooms are threatening ground.

So passionate is the debate that reform is threatened with paralysis by analysis. No single educational philosophy can be expected to win the day in a country as heterogeneous as the U.S. What might work in a high-income suburban school district could create havoc in an inner-city ghetto. And there are no quick fixes. "Imagine a business . . . with 50 totally autonomous divisions and 16,000 subsidiaries, each with its own board of directors and labor agreements," says retired Procter & Gamble Chairman Owen B. Butler. "No effort to change that culture can be expected to succeed in five years."

Whether it's traditionalism or radical reform, better schools require more and better teachers. And here there is trouble. Morale among teachers, who are poorly paid and garner little esteem, is at low ebb. For years the numbers of college students entering teaching has been in decline, and those who do choose teaching often come from the bottom quartile of their college class. The shortage is acute for teachers of math and science and for the minority teachers desperately needed in poor communities as role models.

Increasing pay can help recruit and retain teachers. But so far efforts in that direction have raised average starting salaries only to the $18,000 range—hardly enough to entice talented students away from other professional tracks. A few school districts, though, now pay their best or most experienced teachers several times that amount.

To attract more teachers, New Jersey is experimenting with alternatives to the standard-certification route so that college graduates in fields other than education can come aboard. Using audiovisual aids, computers, satellite teaching, team-teaching, and even switching to staggered semesters can cut down the number of teachers required as well.

Moving teachers who have been promoted into management jobs back into classrooms could be one solution to the labor shortage. School systems are notoriously bureaucratic. According to the AFT, from 1975 to 1986 school districts hired one curriculum adviser, program director, or other desk worker for every new classroom teacher. "Before we ask for additional funds, we must reorder our priorities," says Mary Hatwood Futrell, president of the National Education Association (NEA).

How to shrink staff and administrative functions isn't the only thing schools can learn from business. Incentive pay can also help. In Rochester, N.Y., last year, the teachers' union sat down with administrators to bargain for school-based decision-making and pay hikes of more than 40%. The new contract also established a career ladder with a top rung of so-called lead teachers who can earn up to $70,000 per year in the contract's third year. Top pay requires them to accept assignments in the system's toughest schools, now often in the hands of novice teachers. "They'll be the Clint Eastwoods of teaching," says union head Urbanski.

Reaching disadvantaged kids in tough neighborhoods also may require expanding the traditional role of schools—the only stable institutions in some kids' lives. A handful of inner-city schools are trying on-site day care for teenage mothers, after-school hours to increase learning time, and intensive anti-dropout counseling. Arkansas, New York City, California, and Minnesota have started prekindergartens for four-year-olds. "Pedagogic reforms are wasted unless you do something about social-capital building," says Primerica CEO and social activist William S. Woodside.

Northeastern University economist Andrew Sum argues that an extended school year, which the Japanese have shown benefits middle-class pupils, can do even more for poor kids who, left to home and peer influences, tend to lose ground in summer. California is moving to year-round schools to increase learning time—and to handle a shortage of classroom space.

Sar Levitan of George Washington University believes schools must assume even more roles to fill the gap left by working mothers. "I'm not a moralist, I'm only an economist," Levitan says. "If women are going to do society's work, the schools must respond."

One way to make the schools more responsive to the needs of the students is to force them to compete for students. Some 20 years ago economist Milton Friedman, a Nobel prizewinner, proposed issuing vouchers to families for the amount it costs to educate their kids. Parents would select among the schools, "paying" with the vouchers, so schools would have to upgrade or lose funding.

Although no school system has yet issued a Friedman voucher, there is growing support for the idea of parental choice to foster competition, accountability, and parental involvement. The National Governors' Assn. believes that choice within the public schools "can promote equity." Poor kids, claims Heritage Foundation analyst Jeanne Allen, would benefit most, since wealthier families already choose schools by moving to communities with good ones.

In the past, though, choice has sometimes been used to thwart integration. In some places, so-called magnet schools—the best schools in the district—skim off the community's best students, leaving other schools worse off. "You don't improve schools by running away from schools," bristles NEA President Futrell. Minnesota's teachers are suing their state over its new Choose-a-School plan, which lets kids enroll in any public school.

Other experiments are on the way. Boston University is taking on the reorganization of the troubled Chelsea (Mass.) school system. New Jersey has begun a hostile takeover of Jersey City schools, whose performance was close to meltdown. But much of the system still is plagued with inertia and institutional rigidity. If there is to be meaningful reform, adversaries in the education community will have to cede cherished turf and cooperate.

The alternative—bumbling along from crisis to crisis while presiding over decline—is simply not acceptable. Schools are the crucible where children do or don't become productive members of the community. For children growing into citizens—and for a society that wants to prosper—education is just too important to entrust to the status quo.

THE PUBLIC SCHOOLS AND THE PUBLIC MOOD[2]

In a historic meeting at Charlottesville, Virginia, last September, President George Bush and the nation's governors promised to revitalize America's public schools by establishing "clear national performance goals, goals that will make us internationally competitive." Their language recalled the document that had inspired school reforms earlier in the 1980s, *A Nation at Risk*. President Reagan's first Secretary of Education, Terrel Bell, a quiet educator from Utah, had been appointed in 1981 under the cloud of a Reagan promise to abolish the department. Insecure in his cabinet position and never the public figure his successor, William J. Bennett, proved to be, Bell was nonetheless determined to do something about the mounting evidence of poor performance in the nation's public schools. He appointed a National Commission on Excellence in Education, whose 1983 report resonated deeply with the public mood.

"Our nation is at risk," the commission warned. "If an unfriendly foreign power had attempted to impose on America the mediocre educational performance that exists today, we might

[2]Article by Carl Kaestle, Vilas Professor of Educational Policy Studies and History at the University of Wisconsin at Madison. Reprinted with permission from *AMERICAN HERITAGE*, volume 41, Number 1. Copyright © 1990 by American Heritage, a Division of Forbes, Inc.

well have viewed it as an act of war. . . . We have, in effect, been committing an act of unthinking, unilateral educational disarmament." This message reverberated through the rest of the Reagan years. It was cited again and again as the nation entered a period of major educational stocktaking, hand wringing, and reform. Within a year several new commissions had echoed its theme. A Twentieth Century Fund task force worried that "by almost every measure—the commitment and competency of teachers, student test scores, truancy and dropout rates, crimes of violence—the performance of our schools falls far short of expectations." The Education Commission of the States said the schools were "adrift," and a report by the Carnegie Foundation said that a "deep erosion of confidence in our schools" was coupled with "disturbing evidence that at least some of the skepticism is justified." Reformers called for higher graduation standards, tougher course content, more homework, better teacher training, and merit pay for teachers. The mass media took up the cry, and television networks ran prime-time documentaries on the school crisis.

This crisis did not come out of the blue. Publicity about declining standardized test scores in the late 1970s strengthened a backlash against open education, open campuses, and easy elective courses—things that people associated with the permissive sixties. Problems like racial segregation and illiteracy had proved difficult to solve, and people were disillusioned with the liberal reforms of a previous generation. Complex and coercive federal and state programs designed to correct discrimination had multiplied in the 1970s, and they taxed the bureaucratic capacity of local schools. Principals' and teachers' decisions about where a given child should be at a given moment were beset by contradictory rules about compensatory education, bilingual education, mainstreaming of the handicapped, and desegregation. Many critics and parents became convinced that traditional academic programs were suffering from neglect.

Respect for American public schools declined. In 1974 Gallup pollsters began asking people to grade the public schools. By 1981 the percentage of people who gave the schools an A or a B had declined from 48 percent to 36 percent while the percentage of people who gave the schools an F or a D nearly doubled, from 11 percent to 20 percent. The combination of a disillusioned public and a powerful group of critics had a dramatic effect. Legislatures in many states passed major education-reform bills: graduation requirements were beefed up, teacher salaries were increased, and a flurry of experimental programs were implemented. Although Secretary Bennett left office in 1988 warning that the schools were "still at risk," and reformers are now busy advocating newer programs for teacher training and for inner-city children, there is no doubt that many states took the first wave of criticism seriously and implemented several of the suggested reforms of the mid-1980s.

This was not the first time in American history that critics aroused an anxious public about the quality and content of public schooling. The schools always have had plenty of critics, but widespread reform has succeeded only when there has been a general crisis of confidence in the schools and reformers have solidified public consensus about what changes are needed. Some efforts to mobilize public opinion have worked; others have not.

The nation was barely born when critics first warned of the terrible condition of schoolhouses and the ignorance of schoolmasters. Schools were "completely despicable, wretched, and contemptible," said Robert Coram of Delaware in 1791, and the teachers were "shamefully deficient." Thomas Jefferson and Benjamin Rush suggested school-improvement schemes at the state level, arguing that the fragile Republic could be preserved only by creating an intelligent citizenry. The public was not impressed, and state legislatures refused to pass school-reform bills. People did not think that government intervention in local education was necessary, and they didn't see an urgent need for improvement. "There is a snail-paced gait for the advance of new ideas on the general mind," complained Jefferson in 1806. "People generally have more feeling for canals and roads than education." Thirty years went by before a successful school-reform movement blossomed.

Horace Mann, whose name became synonymous with that movement, grew up when Massachusetts was beginning to industrialize. Born in 1796 to a struggling farm family in Franklin, Massachusetts, he recalled bitterly the endless hours of work and the hellfire-and-brimstone religion of the local Congregationalist minister. When Mann's brother drowned in a local swimming hole on a Sunday, the minster preached about the eternal damnation of sabbath breakers.

Mann was determined to escape this heartless Puritan religion and the marginal economic position of his family. Under the direction of an eccentric but brilliant itinerant teacher named Barrett, Mann put together a course of study that propelled him into the sophomore class of Brown University. A splendid record there led him to a teaching post at Brown and then to the law school at Litchfield, Connecticut. In 1827 he began his political career as a member of the Massachusetts legislature. By the 1830s Mann was a leading figure in the state senate, supporting economic development through the expansion of railroads, as well as new state institutions like insane asylums and prisons.

Both Mann's distaste for orthodox religion and his desire to shape the developing capitalist economy played a role in his educational views. Appointed secretary of the commonwealth's board of education in 1837, he made public schooling his main focus and led the first successful school-reform movement in American history. When he considered Massachusetts's tiny rural school districts and its burgeoning mill towns, Mann was alarmed by low enrollment and poor attendance, as well as by the shoddy facilities, the short sessions, and the poor quality of teachers. Like the *Nation at Risk* panel of the 1980s, Mann argued that failure to educate all children would sabotage American society: "It is not a fearful thing to contemplate that a portion of our children passed through the last year without the advantages of any school, public or private? What would be said, if we saw a large portion of our fellow citizens treasonably engaged in subverting the foundations of the republic, and bringing in anarchy or despotism?"

Mann had many fellow reformers. In New York a legislative committee complained that public funds for education were "utterly wasted" because "one-third to a half of the pupils were daily absent." A report on Albany's schools complained of "low, vulgar, obscene, intemperate, ignorant, profane and utterly incompetent" teachers. In Vermont the new state superintendent of schools said in 1846 that schoolhouses were in "miserable condition" and that tiny rural districts were the paradise of ignorant teachers." All over the country the call for reform was the same. Schoolhouses were poorly built, poorly equipped, and poorly located; teachers were incompetent and lacked supervision; sessions were too short and attendance too irregular.

Memoirs that describe early-nineteenth-century district schools tell about a year divided into two terms: a few months in the winter for all the children and another in summer for those too young to be working. The students ranged in age from three to eighteen, and all studied in the same room, so teachers relied on endless recitations by small groups and struggled to keep order, some by love or persuasion, most by boxing ears and applying birch switches.

The picture of untrained, overburdened teachers struggling to maintain control and teach the three Rs by rote is confirmed in many memoirs of students as well as teachers. As a little boy in winter school in the Catskills, Warren Burton said his ABCs four time a day for his teacher. "This exercise he went through like a great machine, and I like a little one." Otherwise Burton watched the older children, napped, and fidgeted on the hard bench. In Woonsocket, Rhode Island, Elizabeth Chace remembered that "at twelve years of age I had recited *Murray's Grammar* through perhaps over a dozen times without a word of explanation or application from the book or the teacher."

These old district schools had their supporters and produced some fond memories. They sufficed to teach rudimentary literacy to a large part of the population in a basically rural nation, they accommodated the seasonal need for child labor, they were inexpensive, and local religious preferences were often observed in prayer and Bible-reading lessons. Although attendance was voluntary, the sketchy figures we have suggest that more than 60 percent of school-age children went to school for some part of a term during the early nineteenth century.

This wasn't enough for Mann and his fellow school reformers. By the 1840s the district schools seemed clearly inadequate to answer the troublesome problems that industrialization and immigration posed for the nation. Samuel Galloway called schooling in the state of Ohio "the prostrate cause." Caleb Mills revealed the "humiliating fact" that one-seventh of Indiana's adults were "not able to read the charter of her liberties." In the South a report to the Virginia House of Delegates warned, "It would be a fatal delusion to suppose that under the neglect or decay of education, free institutions could preserve a healthful existence." In North Carolina, the state with the most advanced public school law in the South, reformers complained in the 1850s that some local school committees neglected their duties and others misappropriated school funds.

Everywhere there was resistance to reform from those who opposed increased state involvement, standardization, and higher taxes. In upstate New York an opponent of reform complained that school tax laws authorized some people "to put their hands in their neighbors' pockets." A delegate to the Michigan constitutional convention of 1850 warned that if districts were given the power to tax residents for schools, it would endanger passage of the whole revised constitution. In Massachusetts a legislative committee complained that Horace Mann and his board of education were "the commencement of a system of centralization and of monopoly of power in a few hands, contrary, in every respect, to the true spirit of our demoncratical institutions."

Among Mann's opponents were Congregationalists who saw state regulation of education as a threat to religion in the schools. They joined in an effort to have Mann's position abolished. Mann referred to this opposition as "an extensive conspiracy" and wrote to a friend that "the orthodox have hunted me this winter as though they were bloodhounds and I a poor rabbit." In his journal Mann wrote, "I enter another year not without some gloom and apprehension, for *political madmen* are raising voice and arm against the Board." To Henry Barnard, his Connecticut counterpart, Mann wrote, "Let us go on and buffer these waves of opposition with a stout arm."

School reformers promised not only improved intellectual education but improved morals. They emphasized that moral training was crucial to the republican form of government and to work habits and day-to-day behavior as well. They offered to reduce ethnic and class tensions by providing a common meeting ground and a common culture. And despite a long, hard fight, determined opposition, and some setbacks, they won. Devotion to local control of schools gave way by the mid-nineteenth century to anxieties about immigration and economic change and to conflict between Protestants and Catholics. People realized that a higher level of education was needed for the market-oriented economy that industrialization brought with it. A majority of the public in the North had become disillusioned with untrained teachers, short sessions, and make-shift schoolhouses, so they voted for bigger budgets and more state involvement in supervising education.

By 1860 most Northern states had established school funds, state superintendents of instruction, country supervisors, and summer institutes for teachers. Enrollments continued to rise

even thought schooling did not become mandatory until the late nineteenth century. Small neighborhood school districts were consolidated under townwide school committees, and these committees gradually established longer school sessions and better schoolhouses. The public mood had shifted. The appeal to cultural cohesion and economic progress had succeeded.

There were still dissenters, of course. In the 1870s critics charged that the public schools had not made good on their promises of moral education. Bribery, divorce, crime, disrespect for parents—"this is the condition in which we are after more than half a century of experience of our public-school system," said Richard Grant White in the *North American Review* in 1880. He urged the abolition of all public education about the elementary level. A few years later a U.S. Assistant Attorney General named Zachariah Montgomery wrote a book urging the same policy. Public education was a "monstrous usurpation of parental authority" and should be ended, he declared. Montgomery included testimonials from various Protestant clergy to prove that he wasn't just a champion of Catholic schools, and he argued against the "deep-seated and constantly fomented prejudice in favor of the public-school system, which makes politicians afraid to attack the monster."

These were conservative voices crying in the wilderness, though. Not until the 1890s did the public mood shift enough to foster another major reform movement. The problems of labor strife, immigration, and economic depression had escalated by then, intensifying concerns about whether the public schools were doing an adequate job of moral education and cultural assimilation. In the judgment of many observers, the schools had become stagnant—lifeless bureaucracies for the educators and stultifying memorization factories for the children.

The person most responsible for spreading this view was Joseph Mayer Rice, a New York pediatrician interested in education. In 1892 Rice received an invitation from Walter Hines Page, editor of the monthly opinion magazine *The Forum*, to tour thirty-six cities throughout the United States and to inspect their schools. The resulting series of nine articles, beginning in October 1892, caused a sensation. Starting with New York's schools, Rice lambasted the boredom and passivity of rote learning. "In no single exercise is a child permitted to think. He is told just what to say, and he is drilled not only in what to say, but also in the manner in which he must say it." One of Rice's main complaints was the unscientific nature of teaching, a cry that would echo throughout the subsequent reform movement. "The typical New York city primary school," he said, is a "hard, unsympathetic, mechanical-drudgery school, a school into which the light of science has not yet entered." In Baltimore, Rice noted, "the schools . . . *are almost entirely in the hands of untrained teachers,*" and "political influence appears to play a much greater part in their appointment than merit."

There were a few bright spots. Teachers in Indianapolis showed great sympathy for children's interests (another watchword of the developing reform movement), and in Minneapolis Rice found a system free from politics, staffed by well-trained teachers who engaged children in active, creative work. But mostly Rice's series exposed corruption, mindlessness, and failure. "In nearly every class that I visited," he wrote of Philadelphia's schools, though he could have been speaking about the nation's "the busywork meant little more than idleness and mischief. It was the most aimless work that I have ever found."

School officials, of course, reacted defensively to Rice's findings. One professional journal sneered about the "cheap criticisms and the charlatanism of an alleged expert." But Rice caught the public mood. A new reform movement developed in the 1890s, and its name—progressive education—linked it with the larger political reform movement of the day. Actions were taken to distance the schools from ward politics in large cities. Smaller school boards hired "captains of education" to run urban school systems according to efficient, scientific principles. New schools of education churned out research on motivation, individual differences, and specialized curricula for different children.

Two goals were at the heart of progressive education: efficiency and individual growth. The tension between these goals went unrecognized by many reform enthusiasts, who patched together new ideas and new programs in a general effort to make schools more relevant to the world of work and more responsible to children's individual needs. Others recognized the problem but made the kinds of practical compromises necessary in large school systems. In Seattle, for instance, the superintendent Frank Cooper resisted much of the enthusiasm for factory-like efficiency in the schools, but he still believed that testing and grouping were necessary: "The teacher's greatest problem is to diagnose the individual needs of her pupils and then so to adjust her work that she may be able to give each child the thing that he especially needs."

Many educators embraced scientific efficiency and the industrial metaphor without qualms. Franklin Bobbitt, an influential education professor at the University of Chicago, argued that education was like industry: "Whether the organization be for commerce or for manufacture, philanthropy or education . . . the fundamental tasks of management, direction, and supervision are always about the same." He hoped that the business world "would state in specific terms the kind of educational product that it desires," just as railroad companies specify what kinds of rails they need from steel plants.

Meanwhile, John Dewey was advocating a very different version of progressive education. A Vermont farm boy trained in philosophy at Johns Hopkins University, Dewey had already proved himself a brilliant philosopher and a powerful teacher at the University of Michigan when he became head of both philosophy and education at the new University of Chicago in 1894. In the university's Laboratory School, Dewey and his associates tried to provide education that balanced the children's interests with the knowledge of adults, that engaged the children in cooperative, active work, and that integrated social and intellectual learning. The concepts of growth and active learning imbued the curriculum. Children learned about earlier societies through studying people's productive activities. In 1906, for example, the eight-year-olds of the Laboratory School were stydying Phoenician civilization. "The occupational work centered around the trading and maritime activities of the Phoenicians," wrote one of the teachers, "and then moved on to the larger topic of world exploration and discovery." Teachers tried to relate all the work the class did to the Phoenician unit. "As each group passed from home room to shop, to laboratory, to studio, to music room, the things they did or expressed, related to or illustrated as far as possible the activities that went on in the historical study they were dramatizing." This is what Dewey meant by education's involvement with "occupations."

Outright occupational training was something altogether different. When David Snedden, a curriculum expert at Columbia's Teachers College, advocated separate vocational high schools for further factory workers, Dewey debated him in the pages of *The*

New Republic. Dewey objected to the "acquisition of specialized skill in the management of machines at the expense of an industrial intelligence based on science and a knowledge of social problems and conditions." He wanted the kind of knowledge that would "make workers, as far as may be, the masters of their own industrial fate." Chicago labor unions joined the battle, complaining that dual school systems were designed to put the education of working class children "under the complete control of corporations," with the aim of turning out "meek little manikins." Separate schools for vocational education were defeated in Illinois, as in most other places. Despite the vogue of efficient education for industrial productivity, the most extreme schemes failed because they sounded too undemocratic.

The "child-centered" school also encountered opposition, not only from Dewey himself, who considered it too permissive, but also from many parents and teachers. When the public schools in Greenwich Village, New York City, began a progressive elementary school in the 1920s, an Italian mother in the parent-teacher association complained: "The program of that school is suited to the children of well-to-do homes, not to our children. We send our children to school for what we cannot give them ourselves, grammar and drill. . . . We do not send our children to school for group activity; they get plenty of that in the street." Not surprisingly, the New York experiment was soon canceled. Indeed, in the decades that followed, educators adopted efficiency-minded reforms more enthusiastically than child-centered reforms. By the 1950s attempts to combined efficiency and individual development had resulted in an intellectually weak program called Life Adjustment Education. The time was again ripe for school reform, and two conservative strains of criticism—the right-wing anti-Communists of the McCarthy years and the academic traditionalists—emerged to provide it. The anti-Communists knew more about what they didn't like (any liberal textbook or leftist teachers' union) than about what they wanted. In Tenafly, New Jersey, parents identified 131 library books that "follow the Communist line and . . . are written by Communist sympathizers," one of a rash of such attacks in the early 1950s. A number of right-wing organizations sprang up to promote and distribute such publications as *Progressive Education is REDucation*. In Council Bluffs, Iowa, the former congressman Charles Swanson was upset by textbooks that listed Thomas Jefferson, Andrew

Jackson, and Franklin Roosevelt as great Presidents but not William Howard Taft. These books, he said, "should be thrown on a bonfire—or sent to Russia."

The time in the limelight of the obsessed anti-Communists was brief. The champions of traditional academic learning, however, became a considerable voice. They assaulted everything they thought progressive education stood for: a low priority for intellectual training, time wasted on trivial social topics, and an endless string of worthless education courses for teachers. (They often confused John Dewey's original and demanding philosophy with that of his much more permissive and fuzzier disciples.)

A spate of books in the first half of the decade voiced these complaints. The titles tell the story: *Quackery in the Public Schools, The Diminished Mind, The Miseducation of American Teachers, Let's Talk Sense about Our Schools*, and *The Public School Scandal*. The most widely debated book was Arthur Bestor's *Educational Wastelands: The Retreat from Learning in Our Schools*. Bestor, a respected historian of nineteenth-century utopian communities, taught at the University of Illinois. So did Harold Hand, a professor of education and one of the leading defenders of Life Adjustment Education. The two could hardly have been more different. Bestor was the epitome of the college professor; he was reserved, dressed conservatively, and spent his free time in the library. Hand was an outdoorsman and amateur pilot who wore work boots and open shirts, a self-conscious man of the people, yet highly regarded by his colleagues for his intelligence and judgment. His willingness to depart from traditional subject matter stemmed from his experience as a young boy in school in the Dust Bowl in the 1930s, listening to a teacher reading Tennyson's *The Lady of the Lake* while outside, through the window, he could see the topsoil blowing away.

It was a classic confrontation. The two advocates were personally gracious toward each other, but their views were irreconcilable. Hand was convinced that Life Adjustment Education was a necessary and democratic response to the ever-increasing number of young people who were going to high school. Bestor would have none of it. He gave himself over wholly to the debate, dropping his scholarly work and mounting a campaign to convince the public that education profesors had expelled traditional learning from the schools. Unlike some of the other antiprogressive traditionalists, Bestor did not blame the abandonment of traditional learning on Dewey. In fact, he said that progressive education had been "on the right track" up through the 1920s, when he himself had gone to the Lincoln School, a showcase of progressive education at Columbia's Teachers College. But then too many educators forgot about Dewey's efforts to balance the child's interests with a concern to impart traditional knowledge. Life Adjustment Education emphasized social rather than intellectual learning, especially for students with average or low academic ability. This, fumed Bestor, "declares invalid most of the assumptions that have underlain American democracy." Like conservatives in the 1980s, Bestor took the high ground on the issue of democracy: All students should have the same highly academic curriculum, in order to make opportunity equal, convey high expectations, and prepare students for intelligent citizenship.

No doubt Bestor exaggerated the loss of traditional academic subjects in most schools, and he overestimated the power of education professors. Hand argued vociferously that *Educational Wastelands* was full of "falsehoods and misleading statements" as well as "sleight-of-hand" and "bloopers." But Bestor found a receptive audience for his complaints, and he got widespread publicity. In the Life Adjustment curriculum, Bestor complained, "trivia are elaborated beyond all reason," and to prove it, he cited details about helping students develop hobbies and choose a dentist.

Bestor's biting criticism, however, got more publicity than his program for reform. He called for the abolition of the undergraduate education major so that all teachers would get a liberal education. He also argued that experts should have more say in curriculum decisions, hoping that this would lead to a restoration of the traditional disciplines in the schools. And of course he wanted higher standards and tougher exams for students.

Whether this conservative program would have resulted in a successful reform movement simply on the strength of its critique of Life Adjustment Education is doubtful. In any case, it had not done so by October 1957, when the launching of the Russian space satellite *Sputnik* dramatically raised American's anxieties about the Cold War. Many Americans erroneously viewed the satellite as evidence that the Russians had a generally superior school system. Adm. Hyman Rickover wrote that *Sputnik* proved that the Russian schools caused "all children to stretch their intellectual capacities to the utmost." President Eisenhower called upon the schools to give up the path "they have been following as a result of John Dewey's teachings." And *Life* ran a series on the hardworking Alexei Kutzkov, who studied difficult math and science in a Moscow high school and did homework most of the time when he wasn't in a museum. Kutzkov was contrasted with two American children: goofy Steve Lapekas from Chicago, who had fun in school and spent most of his after-school hours fooling around, and Barry Wichmann of Rockwell City, Iowa, the neglected genius with an IQ of 162, whose school had no time, no concern, and no competence to deal with his talents.

With *Sputnik* as the catalyst, Americans launched into a period of frenetic educational reform, led by James Conant and Jerome Bruner. Conant, a former Harvard president and a prestigious spokesman for public education, had an answer to the dual demands of democracy and the Cold War: large comprehensive high schools that grouped students primarily according to ability. Bruner, the premier psychologist of education in the country, gathered some university experts and a smattering of school people at Woods Hole on Cape Cod to talk about the structure of the disciplines and then wrote a landmark book, *The Process of Education*, which inspired new curricula in mathematics and science. The federal government joined the reform movement with a major new initiative, the National Defense Education Act of 1958, which bolstered math, science, and foreign-langauag training at every level. Again, a successful educational-reform movement had resulted when political and social anxieties coincided with a public perception that the schools were not in tune with the needs of the society.

The curriculum reforms of the late 1950s and early 1960s had a special focus on math, science, and talented children. By the mid-1960s these concerns had been overtaken by another shift in the public mood. The civil rights movement, dramatized by the grassroots efforts of blacks and encouraged by the Johnson administration, resulted in a major effort to address poverty and racial prejudice through government action. Education was assigned a key role in this effort, just as it had been assigned a key role in solving the national problems brought about by industrialization in the 1840s, immigration and urbanization in the early 1900s, and the Cold War in the 1950s.

The momentum lasted until the early 1970s. Gaps between the basic skills of minority and majority students narrowed among younger students; a revolution in school integration occurred, particularly in the South; schools recognized and institutionalized the rights of women, the disabled, and non-English-speaking students. But by the mid-1970s the public's tolerance for the disruptions of new programs and regulations was exhausted. Even before Reagan's electoral victory, education officials in the Carter administration were winding down massive student-aid programs, going more slowly on rights enforcement, and reducing the tangle of regulations and reporting required of local districts. A grassroots back-to-basics movement, declining college-entrance-exam scores, economic recession, and foreign competition set the stage for Terrel Bell and his Commission on Excellence in Education. The pendulum had swung again.

Major reforms of public education seem to come in cycles. Some people characterize the swings as conservative or liberal. The progressive decades of 1895 to 1915 and the 1965–75 reform movement are "liberal," meaning that they emphasized equal access to education and recognition of student diversity; the 1950s and the 1980s are "conservative" because they place an emphasis on the nurturing of standards, talent, and traditional academic knowledge. Swings of reform might also be seen as alternating between periods of centralization and professionalization (as in the 1840s, the progressive era, and the 1960s), and periods of resserted localism, private initiative, and challenges to the education establishment (as in the 1950s and the 1980s).

The cycles of public-school reform in our history have had limited effects compared with their goals. They did not achieve full equality of opportunity, harmonious social relations, effective character education, universal literacy, and satisfactory levels of academic excellence. The links between policy makers and teachers in the classroom have always been weak, and schools are rather inert institutions. They have limited resources of time and money to devote to change. Perhaps it is a good thing that schools don't swing radically from one reform agenda to another, but it is frustrating to reformers—both "conservative" and "liberal"—when they try to assess the impact of their heartfelt efforts.

Nonetheless, even if school reforms have limited effects and run in somewhat predictable pendulum swings, they serve two very useful purposes. They force educators to think about what they are doing to defend it, to fine-tune it, and to think about the whole enterprise they are engaged in, not just their specific daily roles. More important, school reforms encourage the public to think about public education—not just about its failings but about its purpose and its importance. To the extent that schools respond successfully to widespread reform sentiment, they give people a sense of having a stake and a voice in the conduct of public schools.

The metaphor of the pendulum is probably too tame for the intense difficulties our public schools will face in the 1990s as reformers try to fashion a movement that addresses the unfinished agenda: dropouts, the problems of low-income and single-parent families, the restructuring of teacher training and teachers' working conditions, the debate over common learning for a highly diverse population, the consolidation of equal rights that have been promised but imperfectly granted, drugs, and, most important, more effective instruction, both in basic skills and in problem solving.

At Charlottesville, President Bush said that "the American people are ready for radical reforms." The next few years will tell how long that mood can be sustained. Meanwhile, school reformers have their work cut out for them.

U.S. EDUCATION: FAILING IN SCIENCE?[3]

U.S. science and math education at the primary and secondary levels is foundering, according to two new surveys released last week by the National Science Foundation. Preliminary results from one survey comparing students' science and math achievement in 17 countries ranked U.S. students fair to poor. A second, U.S.-only study identified worrisome trends in both the nation's teaching practices and its science-teacher education.

[3]Article by Janet Raloff. Reprinted with permission from *Science News*, N 12 '88. 133:165-6. The weekly newsmagazine of science, copyright 1988 by Science Service, Inc.

The multi-nation study, conducted by the International Association for the Evaluation of Educational Achievement, an association of research centers, compared students' performance on special standardized tests at the roughly fifth-, ninth- and twelfth-grade levels. The study looked at approximately 150 students at each of these levels in each country. While U.S. fifth-graders ranked eighth among 15 responding nations, U.S. ninth-graders tied with those in Thailand and Singapore for fourteenth place in a field of 17 responding nations.

But these are grade levels at which all students are taking the same courses. What about the high-achieving science "specialists"—high school seniors taking an optional second year of advanced biology, chemistry or physics? Among the 13 countries responding—Australia, English-speaking Canada, England, Finland, Hong Kong, Hungary, Italy, Japan, Norway, Poland, Singapore, Sweden and the United States—U.S. students placed last in biology, eleventh in chemistry and ninth in physics.

What should concern U.S. education policymakers, says Richard N. Wolf of Teachers College at Columbia University in New York City, who was one of the survey's two U.S. coordinators, is "this apparent progressive decline" in science achievement: from the middle-ranking younger grades—which include even below-average students—to older science specialists.

Bill C. Aldridge, executive director of the Washington, D.C.-based National Science Teachers Association, describes the low rankings given the best U.S. science students as "pretty distressing." Nevertheless, he says, their international standing "is very easy to understand if you look at the other [nations'] curricula." Topping the survey's list for twelfth-grade science specialists were Hong Kong, England and Singapore—nations where these students take only science and math courses. Such curricula are in sharp contrast to a more varied training given U.S. students. (Wolf, who studied this "two-cultures phenomenon" in British Commonwealth countries, says he found that by offering only literature or science in upper grades, "you often had scientists who were illiterate or humanists who were innumerate.")

But most science-education analysts don't think course offerings explain the whole disparity in scores. Many point to other potential cofactors described in the U.S. study involving 6,156 teachers, authored by Iris Weiss, formerly with Research Triangle Institute in Research Triangle Park, N.C. (and now the head of Horizon Research Inc., a consulting firm in Chapel Hill, N.C.). Looking at how teacher training and science/math teaching have changed over the past 10 years, Weiss found several disturbing trends.

Chief among them, she believes, is that teachers are spending more time lecturing their classes and less time on hands-on projects. "This is exactly contrary to what scientists and science educators recommend," she told *Science News*. In 1977, she points out, on any given day roughly 60 percent of classes would involve laboratory work and about 70 percent would include lectures. Now only about 40 percent are doing hands-on work on any given day, while some 80 percent include lectures. She found that elementary grades are more likely to include hands-on training and less likely to involve lectures than either junior high or high school classes.

Even more important, Weiss believes, is the actual amount of time spent on hands-on work. In kindergarten through sixth grade, a science class spends just about as much time (28 percent) on hands-on activity as on lectures (25 percent). But by junior high, an average of 11 percent more classroom time is devoted to lecture than to hands-on activities. By high school, lecturing accounts for 43 percent of the class time—more than twice the time devoted to laboratory studies.

Weiss was also "astonished" at the low classroom use of computers. While virtually every school in the study had computers, she says, only 8 to 15 percent of science classes and 19 to 23 percent of math classes studied had used them in the week prior to the survey. Moreover, of the classes that had used them, most had logged in a total of only 15 minutes or less during that week.

Finally, her data showed that unexpectedly large proportions of high school science and math teachers have an actual degree in science or math (76 and 52 percent respectively)—not just science or math education. However, a third of the chemistry classes and half of the physics classes were taught by individuals who had studied a different field—usually biology. Weiss considers this quite troubling. "Teachers are being trained as if they're only going to teach one subject," she says. Perhaps, she suggests, they should sacrifice some depth of training for some background in a second scientific field.

While conceding that most analysts recommend focusing initial corrective action on the youngest students in the U.S. educational system, F. James Rutherford, chief education officer for the Washington, D.C.-based American Association for the Advancement of Science, believes this is not the way to address such a systemic problem. "I won't be happy," he says, "until we're attacking the problem on all fronts."

HOW TO SMARTEN UP THE SCHOOLS[4]

So ignorant and benighted are many young recruits to the U.S. work force that one executive after another has recoiled in horror, gasping with astonishment. These are the troops we're supposed to win the global competition with? How can such a work force dominate the knowledge-intensive industries where the future will be made? What use are modern management techniques that draw on the worker's talents and initiative when he has no dogged, practical Yankee ingenuity to tap? And if two of every five new jobs that the Labor Department expects to be created by the turn of the century will call for more than basic skills, where will the ten million qualified workers come from to fill them? Presumably not all from Hong Kong.

Little wonder that many executives are joining the education reform movement sweeping America. They fear that if we can't count on public schools to produce workers who can read, think, calculate, and communicate, we can kiss our economic preeminence goodbye.

The failure of U.S. public education from kindergarten through high school is vast and ominous. Its most notorious measure is the plunge in College Board test performance. Combined scores on the verbal and math exams fell almost yearly from 980 points out of a possible 1600 in 1963 to a nadir of 890 in 1980, before gradually recovering to 906 by 1986. On another series of national tests, science performance of 9-, 13-, and 17-year-olds worsened steadily from 1970 to 1982, the last year for which data

[4]Reprint of an article by Myron Magnet, *Fortune* staff writer. *Fortune*, 117:86–90+. Copyright © 1988 by *Fortune*. Reprinted with permission.

are available. Math performance by 17-year-olds has also deteriorated.

Comparison with other nations disheartens. U.S. eighth-graders on an international math test in 1982 answered an average of only 46% of the questions correctly, compared with top-scoring Japan's 64%. The American kids couldn't even top the average score (52%) for the 11 competing nations. Worse, the top 5% of the U.S. 12th-graders who took international calculus and algebra tests in 1982 came in dead last among the top 12th-graders of nine developed countries, squelched not only by first-ranked Japan but also by Finland, New Zealand, Hungary, and others. That 5% is the *crème de la crème*, since few enough U.S. high school seniors take advanced math at all. Contends University of Illinois education professor Herbert J. Walberg: "People often say that our best and brightest can compare with Japan's best and brightest—who only memorize. But it's simply not true."

How literate are American students—not in the sense of being able to declaim Shakespeare or write like George Will, but rather being able to understand an instruction manual or compose a comprehensible memo for the suggestion box? A congressionally mandated study found in 1984 that fewer than a fifth of approximately 2,000 11th-graders could adequately write a note applying for a summer job at a swimming pool. The average 11th-grader, who only just made it into the realm of meaningful discourse, couldn't do a wide range of writing tasks well enough to ensure he would be understood.

Not surprisingly, average young adults are weak readers and reasoners too—but the scope of what they can't do takes your breath away. Of 23,000 young adults who took a simple qualifying exam for entry-level jobs at New York Telephone, 84% flunked. A government-sponsored study estimated that only 37% of the 21- to 25-year-olds tested could be counted on to comprehend material as complex as a *New York Times* article on the downing of KAL Flight 007. Just 38% could dependably carry out such tasks as using a chart to pick the right grade of sandpaper or figuring their change from $3 if they had a 60-cent cup of soup and a $1.95 sandwich. Don't expect more than one young adult in five to read a schedule well enough to say when a bus will reach the terminal.

Reform leaders—executives, governors, educators, and [then] Secretary of Education William J. Bennett and his staff—

are worried not just because many young Americans lack the basic skills needed to build quality cars or even run cash registers. Many new graduates also lack a solid core of the knowledge that makes America work as a country, that common culture that turns a pluralistic hodgepodge into a unified nation without depriving anyone of his distinctive identity. They lack that modicum of political judgment, based on at least a smattering of history, that makes democracy authentic and not a masquerade. Missing too is the historical and literary knowledge that shows the vastness and variety of human aspiration and achievement, strengthening character and values and enlarging one's sense of the possibilities and worth of one's life.

How much is missing grows dismayingly clear from a recent influential book, *What Do Our 17-Year-Olds Know?* by former assistant secretary of education Chester E. Finn Jr. and Columbia Teachers College professor Diane Ravitch. Based on tests of a representative national sample of 8,000 17-year-olds, the book reports that fewer than a third of these high school seniors knew in which half-century the Civil War occurred, or what the Magna Carta is or the Reformation was, or that the Declaration of Independence is the document that marked the separation of the colonies from Britain, or that Lincoln wrote the Emancipation Proclamation. A third of them—this is not a joke—didn't know that Columbus discovered America before 1750 or what *Brown* v. *Board of Education* was about. A third couldn't recognize the best-known passage from either the Constitution or the Declaration of Independence. Just over half knew that Stalin led Russia in World War II and—wait for it—that Russia did not invade Israel during that conflict.

Literature questions uncovered a vaster wasteland of ignorance. For these kids, the modern novel is deader than Marley's ghost: Fewer than one 17-year-old scholar in five could match Dostoevski or Conrad or James Joyce with appropriate book titles, and Hemingway and D. H. Lawrence fared little better. Since each question carried four possible answers—and "I don't know" was not among them—this is a worse result than random guessing would produce and suggests an almost militant ignorance. Fewer than half the students knew that Byron, Keats, and Wordsworth were poets.

More happily, the average student scored 68% on the Shakespeare questions and 67% on the Bible ones—poor enough, but passing grades compared with a flunking average for the tests as a whole. As for the Greek myths also central to our cultural heritage, just over half the students knew who Oedipus was or what an Achilles' heel is. Fewer than half could identify Don Quixote or the main theme of *Walden* or the author of a well-worn pair of Poor Richard's maxims.

How did America com to commit "unthinking, unilateral educational disarmament," as the Department of Education's attention-grabbing *Nation at Risk* report termed it? To begin, blame that tattered orthodoxy, "progressive" education. Repeatedly discredited, it nevertheless doesn't die, thanks primarily to the schools of education that are its life-support apparatus. Whatever freshness might once have sparkled in its child-centered approach, its commitment to social utility and "effective living," its rejection of the tyrannies of facts and memorization, of pressure and competitiveness, that freshness has long since turned to stone.

Just one example of the aridity: the "expanding environments" social studies curriculum most schools use from kindergarten through the third grade. Proceeding like those addresses young children write that move from "Mary Jones, Elm Street" to "U.S.A., the Earth, the Universe," this program starts with the child as a family member and moves through his membership in a school, neighborhood, community, even (inevitably) a global community. The four-year sequence, says education professor Ravitch, "is virtually content-free."

For children living at the end of the 20th century—viewers of TV news, observers of modern life, some even visitors to outer space via *Star Wars* or *E.T.* on the VCR—the triviality of this curriculum anesthetizes the mind. "You belong to a family," explains a popular, representatively vacuous first-grade text analyzed by University of Georgia education professors A. Guy Larkins and Michael L. Hawkins. "Some families have two parents . . . Families do things together." Ditto for families in Canada, England, and Japan—the global approach, you see, based on the belief that if we all stress the many things we have in common instead of our supposedly unimportant differences and conflicts, there would be no wars.

Other equally empty textbooks add that children have birthdays, birthdays are fun, and American Indians and Chinese people have them too. Third-graders—these are 8-year-olds—

soporifically discover that "all communities have homes . . . buildings where people work, play, learn, and worship . . . parks where people go to have fun . . . stores where people shop . . . roads." All four grades learn how milk gets from the cow to the kitchen, each time with the same numbing simple-mindedness. When Benjamin Franklin appears in one book, it is as a Philadelphia post-office improver and college and library founder. Children aren't told he was a diplomat and nation builder, community roles evidently too heady and interesting for the environment expanders who compiled this text.

Obvious, superficial, and unfailingly boring, the Georgia professors judge, these wan texts utterly displaced red-blooded fare that put muscle on children's minds and imaginations—Greek myths, Robinson Crusoe, stories of national heroes like Washington and Lincoln, of Pilgrims, Indians, and pioneers, of heroes of legend and history from Moses and Ulysses to King Arthur and Joan of Arc. Says Diane Ravitch of this older curriculum: "Children *enjoy* it. They learn painlessly when their lively minds and their sense of romance and adventure are engaged." And they learn something other than that school is dumb.

The progressive preference for utility and "effective living" over the inspiring and instructive richness of our cultural heritage works its way all through the curriculum and powerfully shapes what high-schoolers learn, or don't learn. These days cooking and driving courses count as much toward a high school diploma as English, history, or science courses. While it's fine to teach kids to cook and drive, 13 states let high-schoolers earn at least half their graduation credits from electives like these or like Bachelor Living, where presumably they can learn condom etiquette and that communities have singles bars.

Though progressive education has been doing its work for more than 60 years, it took the upheavals of the Sixties and early Seventies to exaggerate all its tendencies and hasten the evacuation of learning from the schools. A revealing case in point: the trivialization of American history textbooks. While schoolbook publishers are used to dancing tactfully among the sometimes contradictory demands of text-buying authorities wedded to fundamentalism or secular humanism or the free market, the contentions of the Sixties overwhelmed their suavity. That became clear in a report of an expert panel sponsored by the New York-based Educational Excellence Network.

With blacks, Hispanics, American Indians, other ethnic groups, feminists, homosexuals, and nuclear disarmers all clamoring for due mention of the dignity of their accomplishment or injustice of their suffering, history books have resorted to what the report calls "a kind of textual affirmative action." This often crowds out the more important parts of the story and turns texts into dead catalogues of disjointed facts or "distort[s] in order to mention and appease." In the pictures in one leading high school text, the report says, "Texas cowboys, World War I soldiers, and Civilian Conservation Corps surveyors are represented [only] by blacks. In its index, Women's Rights is a longer entry than the Revolutionary War."

Since such texts must not offend interest groups, you can guess how forceful the writing is. Deadly too is that the committees that write these books prefer thinking sociologically about communities and social classes rather than thinking in the traditional historical terms of stories filled with passion and conflict and peopled by vivid characters whose bold or devious or wise actions change the world. So much for drama. Since the texts mustn't use too difficult a vocabulary or carry too heavy a "concept load," they end up even more vapid and colorless.

Progressive education has always tried to replace teacher authoritarianism with teacher-pupil cooperation. But the Sixties' shakeup of education reduced the distance between teacher and pupil so drastically that it fatally subverted teacher authority. Teachers lost confidence that they really knew what pupils should learn, even that they as teachers had something worth teaching. Popular songs might well contain as much wisdom and poetry as Melville, went the cant of the day, and spontaneity might be more valuable than knowledge.

At the college level, where this tendency was most pronounced, the consequence was a reduction in course requirements and admission requirements. High schools in turn reduced graduation requirements, figuring that if colleges didn't require applicants to know foreign languages or sciences for admission, maybe they weren't important. Trivial electives and texts crowded out solid fare in the name of a specious relevance, so that today, 20 years later, students read a biography of onetime teen tennis player Tracy Austin, say, instead of the life of Marie Curie or Pocahontas.

Required homework went the way of required courses. The proportion of high school seniors who did at least five hours a week declined 30% between 1972 and 1980. Says assistant education secretary Finn: "Kids tend to learn that which they study, and to learn it in proportion to the amount of study they do—and up to the level they are obliged to learn it to by the adults in their lives." Not only does less homework produce less learning, but it also fails to instill the work ethic that the U.S. economy needs. Even as teachers were demanding less from students in every way, they were inflating grades, further eroding the incentive to work hard.

Such authority as the schools left themselves the courts helped take away. Principals cannot suspend pupils without a formal hearing, the Supreme Court ruled in 1975, invoking the 14th Amendment's due-process guarantee and thereby turning school discipline from an extension of parental discipline into a quasi-adversarial proceeding on the legal model. Weeks later the Court subverted school order further by ruling that pupils could sue individual teachers and principals for damages for infringing their civil rights. How much do you want to discipline a troublemaker who can make a federal case of it?

The Court broadly impaired learning with the forced busing that followed its 1971 *Swann* ruling. Views differ on whether busing is sound social policy, but it is hard to disagree that its educational costs have been high. In many districts race relations for years became at least as much the focus of school life as education. Angry mobs, frightened or hostile children, and policemen in school hallways did not foster an atmosphere conducive to learning. For a federal judge like W. Arthur Garrity Jr., who ran the Boston school system like a commissar for 11 years, the first priority could not be education. The white flight that busing accelerated often deprived urban schools of the most motivated pupils, whose mainstream values helped set a tone of order and relative respect for school.

Americans like to think that schools can be used to change society, but the influence goes both ways. From the Sixties onward vast social and cultural changes twisted schools out of shape. Families grew unstable, what with the increasing divorce rate and, in a small sliver of society, an emerging underclass pathology. Says University of Chicago sociologist James Coleman, author of the well-known 1966 Coleman Report on education: "Schools were never successful with children from families who didn't have a high level of educational aspirations and strong support for those aspirations." Faced with an influx of children from weak families, schools reduced their demands. They did so especially since the weak families included minority families who advocates persuaded courts that the high failure and suspension rates among their children were evidence not of pupil shortcomings but of discrimination. Public education reduced itself to the lowest common denominator. Coleman's conclusion: "Weak families have created weak schools, which are not good for kids from strong families." Nor are they good for children from weak families, who arguably need education the most.

If U.S. education were like a run-down factory that required only a little sprucing up and modernizing, the situation wouldn't be so troubling. Instead, with the notable exception of some suburban schools and urban magnet schools, it more resembles an overgrown garden where weeds are beginning to choke out the wholesome growth and supplant it. The forces that have devastated traditional schooling have left not a vacuum but something like a new American culture that is disquietingly resistant to learning.

This culture is producing a new democratic character, minutely anatomized in Allan Bloom's *The Closing of the American Mind*, whose runaway sales attest to the surge of national concern about the bankruptcy of education. At the center of this distinctive modern American personality is a profound belief that truth and values are relative and that therefore the proper attitude toward the world is an indiscriminate openness, a willingness to accept without judging. Students learn this in part from an education whose unthinking global pluralism tells them that different cultures are all much alike deep down, that the differences don't matter, that the most divergent ways of doing and believing and valuing are equally worthy of respect. It is an openness that by making all things equal makes them equally unimportant and therefore not very interesting to learn.

Nothing else in the spirit of this age gives learning any hold on the young. They know that progress has made the past obsolete, with nothing to teach them. They are isolated in a complacent egoism fostered partly by progressive education's emphasis on the child's spontaneous feelings, partly by the emotional remoteness often engendered by the divorce of their parents or the evident impermanence of all the relationships around them, partly by an inability to attach themselves emotionally to a national community that they've been taught is no better than any other one, partly even by their omnipresent rock music's glorification of each adolescent impulse. You can certainly teach such children basics like math and science. But it will take skillful teachers, and especially teachers who are not immersed in this same culture, to get them at all fired up about the rest of our neglected cultural inheritance.

Where to start to fix this mess? The education reformers offer an array of ingenious answers, some of which have begun to sprout programs. Their first helpful idea is that everyone involved—students and especially every level of education authority—must be held accountable for student performance. This means finding out how the students really are doing and publicizing the results. In the individual student learning what he or she is supposed to learn? Twenty-four states make sure by demanding that he or she pass a competency exam for high school graduation, and 11 states require competency exams for promotion from grade to grade. Some states are mindful that a passing grade, designed to represent minimum acceptable performance, can turn into the norm, depressing standards rather than raising them. These states keep the hurdle high.

How do the students of each school perform? Over a dozen states publish a report card that grades and compares schools, allowing taxpayers and parents to hold authorities accountable by opposing higher taxes for schools or by voting out elected administrators or by complaining to teachers and principals. In Prince George's County, Maryland, Superintendent John A. Murphy makes his 172 principals answerable for their pupils' test scores by posting in his conference room bold graphs of each school's annual scores, prominently labeled with the principal's name. Murphy's school reforms get plenty of credit for the recent economic turn-around of this racially mixed area straddling the Washington Beltway. He came into office in 1984 vowing to raise his schools' scores from the 50th percentile range nationwide to the top quarter in 1990. The goals he sets for his principals go up annually in order to meet that mark, which he thinks he will reach a year ahead of schedule.

So far, just knowing that the boss is watching has proved incentive enough. Says he: "As in any business, if you're going to measure people to see whether or not they're performing, they're going to perform—even if you can't reward them." But he already has started talking about including principals and teachers in a bonus pay plan, based—to foster teamwork within each school—on the success of a school's test scores, attendance rates, advanced course enrollment, and so on. Making each school responsible for its own results will of course require moving authority from the central school district bureaucracy to the principal, a move education reformers urge. Says William Kristol, chief of staff to Secretary of Education Bennett: "The problem now is schools are overregulated but underaccountable. We should free up the principal and then reward him if he does well and change him if he does poorly."

Accountability also extends to school boards and school superintendents, who in a handful of states can be placed under the thumb of a state monitor in case of gross incompetence. The Department of Education has been publicizing state-by-state College Board scores, often with the enthusiastic applause of governors. Says Richard P. Mills, chief education aide to New Jersey Governor Thomas Kean: "You cannot be a governor without being an education advocate right now. If you're concerned about regional development, you have to be concerned about the quality of the graduates." Governors have also realized that education is their biggest budget item, swallowing around 40% of state revenues.

You can't get far without improving the quality of teachers. Today's talented young people rarely choose the classroom as a career, especially now that smart, ambitious women are hardly restricted to traditional "women's work" like teaching. Last year's high school seniors who intended to major in education posted combined verbal and math College Board scores of 845, 61 points below the already dismal average of all seniors. Only 58% of these prospective teachers—compared with 68% of all college-bound seniors—had chosen an academic track in high school. The rest took general or vocational programs heavy in courses of the Bachelor Living ilk.

In response, New Jersey has upped admission requirements for the education programs in its state colleges, and Missouri has set up grants and loans designed to attract into teacher-training programs students with high grades and SAT scores. Dismayed by teacher certification exams that often test little more than basic literacy, the Washington-based Carnegie Forum on Education and the Economy has organized a National Board of Professional Teaching Standards, which will issue certificates to teachers who pass the rigorous tests it is now devising. Says foundation executive director Marc Tucker: "You won't need it to get a job at first, but as in every other profession, people will want a board-certified professional."

Universally contemptuous of the education major as a vapid and inadequate program, reformers agree that teachers need a four-year liberal arts education, with a major in whatever subject they plan to teach. The reformers recommend a further year or two learning teaching techniques, perhaps as an apprentice supervised by a master teacher.

New Jersey has proved that teachers educated this way can succeed resoundingly in the classroom. It hires teachers who haven't taken the usual education courses required for certification if they have a BA in the subject they want to teach, can pass the Educational Testing Service's National Teacher Exam in it, and successfully complete a year's residency, which includes a sort of pedagogical boot camp. The 800 teachers New Jersey has hired by these criteria—including retired business and military people, musicians, less well paid parochial school teachers, and recent college grads who have decided they'd like to teach—have higher SAT scores and college grades than teachers with education degrees.

Now New Jersey is trying to set up a new route to the certification of principals. Instead of three years' teaching experience and three specialized courses, you will get certified with an MBA or any master's degree in management. All you'll need to do is take a management test, go through an assessment center, and work for a year under supervision. Wall Street casualties, look across the river.

You can't attract better teachers without increasing their pay. But, says Prince George's superintendent Murphy, "taxpayers are sick and tired of giving across-the-board raises and letting those people who aren't doing the job get more and more money." After all, per-pupil education expenditures between 1950 and 1986, adjusted for inflation, more than tripled to around a breathtaking $4,000, with most of the rise coming in the period when SAT scores plummeted. But taxpayers will tolerate increased spending tied to results, like Murphy's planned performance-based bonus or like Rochester, New York's new teacher career ladder. As teachers grow in competence through four defined ranks, their pay will go up to a peak for the very best of $60,000.

Reformers like to point with fascination to the slums of Spanish Harlem, where Community School District 4 pulled itself from 32nd place out of 32 New York City school districts in test scores in 1973 to 16th today. Students reading at grade level rose from 16% to 63%. The secret: a network of elementary and junior high schools from which parents are free to choose the one they like best for their children, regardless of where they live in the district.

Each school, headed by a director without tenure, has its own distinctive twist—a focus on music or math, say, or a rigorous, traditional curriculum—and so students separate themselves into groups according to their own or their families' ambitions for their future. Each school is small enough so that students aren't anonymous. Directors of these schools make their pitches to prospective students and their parents in the spring before students enter. The market mechanism operates: Schools get better and more various by competing to offer what people want. Those that offer it successfully flourish; the others dwindle.

Warm fans of District 4 include some reformers who favor a voucher system for education. This would let parents send a child to either a public or an accredited *private* school, with the $4,000 or so of tax money earmarked for his education paid out accordingly. Competition would improve all the schools, these reformers say, probably correctly. The need to perform or go out of business would beat down vested interests resisting public school reform—especially the National Education Association, the largest teachers' union, which vehemently opposes merit pay, alternate teacher certification, and teacher competency testing.

But if one object of education reform is to restore a shared cultural core to Americans, the centrifugal tendency of a voucher system seems a push in the wrong direction. The system inevitably would proliferate sectarian schools and so promote separateness rather than commonality. It would be justified as a last resort only if public education were bankrupt beyond repair, or if schools bent on satisfying every interest group developed curricula that were all periphery and no core, or if children who wanted to learn were prevented from getting a decent education by a disruptive population required to attend school. Most public schools haven't reached that point, though, and the reform movement is likely to keep them from it.

A better solution is what California school authorities have been doing to the school curriculum. They have tried to come to grips with just what the core culture includes—that shared national knowledge that E. D. Hirsch Jr. defined in the title of his best-selling book, *Cultural Literacy*. The state education department has drawn up a list of a thousand mainstream books—from *Cinderella* to *Great Expectations*—that ideally children should have read or listened to between kindergarten and high school graduation. The department also has just drawn up an extensive framework for a history and social studies curriculum that will begin in kindergarten with stories about how people lived in the past and with the simplest preliminary discussions of democratic values. From grades five through 12 students will alternate each year between courses in world history and American history, moving from earliest times to the present. California's state testing program will ensure that local schools teach what these curricula prescribe.

Though the history curriculum celebrates cultural diversity, there's nothing relativistic about it; it aims to inspire a high respect for democracy. Unlike a high school in New York's Westchester County that, for fear of offending secularists, failed to tell pupils who was thanked on Thanksgiving, and defined a pilgrim as one who takes a very long journey, the California courses will deal straightforwardly with controversial or difficult issues, explaining their historical significance and outlining the current fuss over them.

Says California superintendent of education Bill Honig: "In a free country, where you have free choice, you have to choose from an educated perspective. Our teachers never make the most important point about education: It helps you lead a better life." If reformers can ensure such an education to the majority of Americans, it will be a famous victory.

A NATION STILL AT RISK[5]

Six years ago, a blue-ribbon commission studying our education system declared us a "nation at risk." Our students were not studying the right subjects, were not working hard enough, were not learning enough. Their schools suffered from slack and uneven standards. Many of their teachers were ill-prepared. "If an unfriendly foreign power had attempted to impose on America the mediocre educational performance that exists today," the panel said, "we might well have viewed it as an act of war." And, it soberly warned, if the United States did not promptly set matters right, our social structure would crack, our culture erode, our economy totter, our national defenses weaken.

To be sure, panels of this sort practically always forcast dire consequences if drastic improvements are not speedily made. But the National Commission on Excellence in Education did not exaggerate. And its voice was not a lone one. An avalanche of studies and reports in the early 1980's drew the same conclusions. It was a time of searching appraisals of American education, and the verdicts were almost uniformly grim.

Nor did they go unheard. Largely thanks to the leadership of crusading "education governors," gutsy state legislators, worried business leaders, and other non-educators, we have had at least a half-decade of efforts to change the practices of the education system in the hope of strengthening its results. Many call this reform wave the "excellence movement." Actually, it is heir to the smaller "back-to-basics" movement of the late 70's, a time when, alarmed by evidence of illiterate high-school graduates, some states adopted "minimum-competency" laws and other measures designed to ensure that those getting diplomas from the public schools would possess at least rudimentary skills in the three R's.

This concern with the output of the education system has proved more durable than anyone expected, and some of the actions taken in its name have been imaginative, more than a few of them courageous. Such terms as "accountability" have gained currency. One state after another has enacted "comprehensive"

[5]Article by Chester E. Finn, Jr., former Assistant Secretary of Education, and currently professor of education and public policy at Vanderbilt University. Reprinted from *Commentary*, My '89. 87:17–23 by permission. All rights reserved.

education-reform legislation, adding to graduation requirements, installing a kindergarten level, shrinking the average class
size, obliging teachers to take literacy exams, making students
pass all manner of tests, rearranging the rules for teacher licens-
ing, experimenting with "school site management," revamping
administrative arrangements, and more.

Such changes cost money, and as a nation we have been paying generously. We have also been raising teacher salaries nearly
everywhere. Though impoverished schools can be found here
and there, and although occasionally a school levy is rejected, the
average per-pupil expenditure in American public education this
year is about $4,800, some $1,500 higher than when *A Nation at
Risk* was released. Today we are spending roughly twice as much
per student in real terms as in the mid-60's, and nearly three
times the level of the mid-50's.

So how, it is fair to ask, are we doing? What have we to show
for these sizable infusions of treasure, energy, and concern? Are
we any less at risk?

In early 1988, a half-decade after the appearance of *A Nation
at Risk*, President Reagan asked then-Education Secretary William J. Bennett to prepare a progress report. It was in Bennett's
interest to paint as rosy a picture as possible. He was, after all,
summing up developments on his and Reagan's watch. Yet here
is what he reported:

American education has made some undeniable progress in the last few
years. . . . We are doing better than we were in 1983.
  But we are certainly not doing well enough, and we are not doing well
enough fast enough. We are still at risk. The absolute level at which our
improvements are taking place is unacceptably low. Too many students
do not graduate from our high schools, and too many of those who do
graduate have been poorly educated. Our students know too little, and
their command of essential skills is too slight. . . . And the entire project
of American education—at every level—remains insufficiently accountable for the result that matters most: student learning.

The long and short of it is that when gauged in terms of student learning—the only outcome that ultimately counts, all else
being means to that end—the results of the excellence movement
to date have been scant. The average student continues to
emerge from the typical school in possession of mediocre skills
and skimpy knowledge.

To be sure, as Bennett suggested, all is not entirely bleak. We are not doing badly at the bottom end. Rudimentary skills are nearly universal. Among those who remain in school and graduate, few today are wholly illiterate. The gap between white youngsters' scores and those of black and Hispanic children has narrowed. We can thus take passing satisfaction from our progress in getting "back to the basics."

Moreover, as always in the vastness of American education with its 100,000 schools, 3,400 colleges, and 58 million students, there are many fine schools and high-achieving youngsters. When the results of the Westinghouse science-talent search come out each winter, a few high schools do wonderfully well. Of the 300 semi-finalists in 1989, Virginia's Thomas Jefferson High School for Science and Technology accounted for 15; New York City schools claimed 105, mainly at the selective Bronx Science and Stuyvesant high schools.

But all this is the exception, and hardly constitutes a plateau to rest on. More typical are recent findings of the National Assessment of Educational Progress and similar barometers:

• Just 5 percent of seventeen-year-old high-school students can read well enough to understand and use information found in technical materials, literary essays, and historical documents.

• Barely 6 percent of them can solve multi-step math problems and use basic algebra. That means correctly answering questions at this level of difficulty: "Christine borrowed $850 for one year from the Friendly Finance Company. If she paid 12 percent simple interest on the loan, what was the total amount she repaid?"

• Only 7 percent are able to infer relationships and draw conclusions from detailed scientific knowledge.

• Sixty percent of eleventh-graders do not know why *The Federalist* papers were written; three-quarters cannot say when Lincoln was President; just one in five knows what "Reconstruction" was about.

• Most high-school students cannot explain what a "government budget deficit" is; two-thirds do not know what "profits" mean.

• Given a blank map of Europe and asked to identify particular countries, young American adults (ages eighteen to twenty-four) typically give the correct answer less than one time in four. Twenty-six percent spot Greece, 37 percent France, just 10 percent Yugoslavia. Asked to do the same thing with American states, fewer than half locate New York and only one in four properly labels Massachusetts.

Such examples are painfully familiar nowadays. We often encounter them in the morning papers and on the evening news. In fact, however, they are but the tip of an iceberg of ignorance. Note, too, that most of the reports from which they are drawn describe young people who have *stayed in school* and are soon to graduate, those commonly deemed to be "succeeding" in our education system. Excluded from the data is the quarter of the teenage population that drops out, slows down, or defers completion of high school.

Looking overseas for points of reference, we find even greater reason for dismay. Every year or so, we get the results of another international study. The most recent, reported by the Educational Testing Service in January, compares the performance of thirteen-year-olds in mathematics and science in six countries. In math, ours came in dead last. In science, American girls and boys were tied for last place (with Ireland and two Canadian provinces). Korea led in both subjects, and the United States was also bested in both by England, Spain, and three other Canadian provinces.

Although my main focus here is on the elementary and secondary schools, the implications for higher education are profound. More than half of our secondary-school graduates enter college right away (and 70 percent commence some sort of postsecondary education within six years). In the population aged twenty-five to thirty-five, the United States now boasts many more college graduates than high-school dropouts, a demographic milestone reached in the 1970's. We award more than 1.8 million additional degrees each year. The scale of our higher-education system is staggering—and unprecedented in the world. But for how many of the young people who swarm into it does "participation in post-secondary education," or even earning a degree, mean acquiring a real "higher" education? The evidence is not encouraging:

• The Southern Regional Education Board recently asked colleges and universities in its fifteen states how many of their entering freshmen were academically unready for higher education. Thirty percent of the institutions reported that this was the case with at least half their new students; on 60 percent of the campuses, remedial work was indicated for at least a third of the freshmen.

• New Jersey administers a basic-skills placement test to all students entering its state colleges and universities. In 1987, just 27 percent of them were found "proficient" in verbal skills, 31 percent in "computation," and only 15 percent in elementary algebra. Even at Rutgers, the flagship, barely half the freshmen could handle elementary algebra and nearly two in five lacked verbal skills.

One might surmise that students unprepared for college at age eighteen will not have acquired a full-fledged "higher" education four years later. Though hard data are scarce, such information as we have suggests that this is indeed the case. Our campuses are conferring degrees on many people whose intellectual skills are still shaky. Reports the National Center for Education Statistics, after analyzing various forms of "literacy" among young adults in 1985:

Among the most highly educated young adults in the nation—those with a four-year college degree—one-half of white young adults and more than 8 out of 10 black young adults were unable to perform at the 350 level of the scales. Tasks characteristic of this level include stating in writing the argument made in a long newspaper column, using a bus schedule to select the bus for given departures and arrivals, and calculating a tip in a restaurant given the tip percentage and the bill.

Finally, if students entering college are inadequately prepared, so are those young Americans who head into jobs rather than through university gates at the end of their secondary schooling. Many employers report acute difficulty hiring skilled and even semiskilled workers. New York Telephone Company, for example, has grown accustomed to a 20-percent pass rate on its test for telephone operators. Motorola has found about the same proportion succeeding on its seventh-grade-level English composition and fifth-grade math tests. By some estimates, companies are spending as much as $60 billion a year on employee training, a huge fraction of this not on specialized job-related techniques but on equipping workers with essential intellectual skills and knowledge, the kind they did not get in school.

Foreign visitors to American schools are often struck favorably by the geniality and helpfulness of the students they meet. Unfortunately, affability is not a sufficient outcome of formal education. To persist on our present course is to continue producing high-school graduates who are amiable but ignorant. It is to keep turning many colleges into remedial high schools, and to continue pouring into the job market millions of young people who do not have what it takes to handle the jobs available to them. And this, of course, means continuing as a nation to fall behind our European and Asian allies, enemies, and rivals.

Why are we not getting better results? Why have so many sincere efforts at reform yielded so little? It is not for lack of concern, not for lack of national self-reproach, and not for want of money. Instead, we have been foundering on three large obstacles, and are on the verge of colliding with a fourth that is the most formidable of all.

The first of the obstacles is widespread denial. Most Americans appear to agree that the nation as a whole is experiencing some sort of educational meltdown, but simultaneously persist in believing that they and their children are doing satisfactorily. One of the questions asked by the international math and science study cited above was whether the thirteen-year-olds who took the test considered themselves "good at mathematics." The American youngsters, while trailing their agemates everywhere in terms of actual proficiency, led the pack when it came to self-regard. Sixty-eight percent answered this question affirmatively, as opposed to just 23 percent in high-scoring Korea.

American parents are reasonably content, too. Harold W. Stevenson of the University of Michigan has spent years comparing the educational performance of elementary-school students in the U.S. with that of youngsters in Taiwan, Japan, and China. The American children lag way behind the others in reading and math. But one would never know this from their mothers' attitudes and opinions. Here are some of Stevenson's findings:

> Not only did American mothers generally have the most favorable evaluations of their children, they also were the most satisfied with their child's current academic performance. . . . Mothers also were asked to evaluate the effectiveness of the schools in educating their children. American mothers were very positive: 91 percent judge the schools as doing an "excellent" or "good" job. This was more than double the percentage of Chinese mothers (42 percent) and Japanese mothers (39 percent) who chose these categories.

Professional educators contribute to the general complacency. Beginning with a generalized "t'ain't so" reaction to *A Nation at Risk*, the profession has spent a fair portion of its energy these past six years arguing that things are not really so bad—and citing data contrived to prove the point. As John J. Cannell has demonstrated, virtually every state and locality in the land that uses standardized tests (i.e., essentially all of them) has managed to find its own students "above average"—and improving. Immediately dubbed the "Lake Woebegon effect," this statistical fantasy results from shrewd test selection, from not "renorming" on a regular basis, from slipshod test security, and perhaps from a bit of plain old cheating.

When denial fails, educators sometimes resort to scapegoating. Thus, when Secretary Bennett issued his five-year appraisal in 1988, the National Education Association promptly termed it a "cover-up for the Reagan administration's failure to help improve America's schools." Ernest Boyer of the Carnegie Foundation for the Advancement of Teaching said Bennett's "divisiveness" was "really sad, if not tragic." Frank Newman of the Education Commission of the States dubbed the report a "major disservice." Gordon Ambach of the Council of Chief State School Officers sniffed that it was a "reheated wall chart out front of the Secretary's rehashed personal agenda." "Did he expect that there was going to be some overnight miracle or something?" fumed Hartford's school superintendent.

The public has thus been lulled for years into thinking that the schools are in pretty decent shape and getting better, if not in the country at large then certainly in their own community. This is surely why the Gallup poll annually shows people giving higher marks to their children's school than to schools-in-general. What is more, the signals parents get from their local schools nearly always indicate that their own children *are* doing satisfactorily—passing grades on their report cards, regular promotion to the next grade. Little do parents know that the standards themselves are lax, that doing well in school is not necessarily the same as learning much, and that it is an article of faith among American educators that "retaining" children is evil.

Second, our reform efforts to date have lacked any coherent sense of exactly what results we are seeking to achieve.

In education, as in any enterprise that strives to turn one thing into another, the normal way to begin is by describing as clearly as possible the product one proposes to create. With specifications in hand, it then becomes possible to design a system that will yield the desired result. If we are clear about the skills, knowledge, habits, and attitudes a young person should possess upon emerging from school into adulthood, practically everything else can be fitted into place: the detailed curriculum, the allocation of resources, the choice of textbooks, the requisites for teaching, the amount of time (which will surely vary) individuals must spend in order to progress through the subordinate levels that accumulate into the eventual result.

A basic failing of education-reform efforts in recent years is that they have tried to work the other way around. We have tinkered endlessly with the production system—its resources, processes, organizational arrangements, and employees—without pausing to specify the product we want to emerge at the other end. The consequence has been a lot of wasted motion.

With goals, of course, must come standards and expectations, or the goals will never be achieved. Most young people learn pretty much what they are obliged to learn by parents and teachers—and in matters academic, not a great deal more. That is why educational norms are so important, especially for disadvantaged youngsters. And that is why uncommonly demanding teachers—like Jaime Escalante, recently portrayed in the movie *Stand and Deliver* and the book *Escalante: The Best Teacher in America*— succeed.

Third, in the absence of clear goals, it has been easy to ignore the primordial finding both of educational research and of common sense: people tend to learn that which they study, and to learn it in rough proportion to the amount of time they spend at the task.

Obvious though this maxim sounds, we have not taken it to heart. A look at the transcripts of the high-school graduating class of 1987—the youngsters who entered high school in the autumn the nation was declared "at risk"—reveals that only 30 percent of them actually took four years of English and three years each of math, science, and social studies. And even this minimalist core was unevenly distributed, with more than half of Asian-American but fewer than a quarter of black and Hispanic youngsters toiling through it.

We know perfectly well that learning takes time and perspiration, yet in our high schools important academic subjects—

history, chemistry, foreign languages—are commonly studied for just a single year, while in other countries they are part of *every* year's curriculum. Moreover, our children have shorter school days and school years than their peers in most of the rest of the industrialized world; they spend far fewer hours doing homework; and big chunks of the typical American school day and class period are given over to nonacademic pursuits, ranging from assembly programs to the time spent passing out and collecting materials.

These three failings are grave. Unchanged, they will keep us from making significant educational gains. Setting them right will be arduous, maybe harder than we have the stomach for. But they are not beyond our capacities to resolve. We can, if we choose, accept the fact that it is *our* children, and the school down the street, that are "at risk." We can become clear about what we desire the education system to produce, and settle upon a satisfactory minimum level of attainment. (Several states and a number of localities are already demonstrating what a core curriculum might look like, and so is the Thatcher government in England.) And we can become much more exacting about performance standards, and more generous with the amount of time and instruction devoted to meeting them.

It is no mystery what needs doing. It is, rather, a matter of the will to do it. But here we come smack up against the fourth obstacle—the one now being rolled into place by the education profession itself.

It begins with the warning, trumpeted by professional educators and their advocates in every medium at their command, that "top-down" changes of the sort urged by commissions, designed by governors, and enacted by legislatures, *cannot* yield significant gains in student learning, and that such moves actually worsen matters by curbing the professional discretion of teachers and turning them into tightly controlled educational mechanics. Instead, we are instructed, the way to make progress is to "empower" teachers and principals to do pretty much as they see fit, school building by school building.

Accompanying these notions is—no real surprise—a demand for still more money for education. The additional outlays are to go mainly for higher salaries and for hiring more teachers, the latter proposal often justified by the desire to reduce class size, begin school at a younger age, and provide more "services," especially for "children at risk."

It is obvious why educators should warm to this set of suggestions—collectively termed the "second reform movement" by Albert Shanker, president of the American Federation of Teachers—and why they have already become the conventional wisdom within the profession, filling the journals, the annual conventions, many union contract negotiations, and myriad faculty meetings at colleges of education. Less clear is why they have caught the eye of a number of elected officials, lay policy-makers, newspaper editorialists, and even business leaders. Perhaps these people have become disheartened by the slow pace of reform; or perhaps they are growing weary of policy combat with the professionals, and are disposed to step aside. In any event, if the new agenda is followed, it will assuredly lead to greater public expenditures on education, endless palaver, and myriad reports and studies. It will also serve to enlarge the professional education industry. But will it do any good for students? Will they actually learn more? No one has the faintest idea, though worthwhile experiments are under way in such places as Miami, San Diego, and Rochester that may eventually shed some light on this question.

Certainly, there is much to be said in principle for cutting back the stultifying central-office bureaucracies of school systems, for recognizing the individual school as the essential unit of educational activity (and accountability), for encouraging schools to distinguish themselves from one another, and for allowing families to choose those that will best serve their children. In these respects, the "second reform movement" contains ideas that ought not to be dismissed. But we dare not romanticize the capacity of the average school, turned loose on its own, rapidly to bring about marked gains in the skills and knowledge of its students. Neither is it prudent to dash off in hot pursuit of an unproven strategy until we have corrected the mistakes in our present plan of attack.

But the biggest reason we ought not to follow the advice of the education profession is that its ideas about the goals of schooling are mostly wrong.

Simply put, the underlying problem we confront as we set about to produce more knowledgeable citizens is that few of our educators have much use for knowledge. The same is true of those who prepare them for classroom teaching, and, by and

large, it is also true of the intellectual elites now propounding
their own notions of how to fix the schools. *This* is the condition
most menacing to the hopes and prospects of school reform.

American education is dominated by the conviction that it is
not really important to know anything in particular. Facts are out.
What is in is exemplified by this recent episode:

A fourth grader is assigned by the teacher to write a report
about the Navaho. The teacher's instructions carefully set forth
the aspects of Indian life that the students are to cover, such as
dress, food, housing, rituals, and transportation.

The boy seeks assistance from his mother, who sensibly begins by asking what era the report is to describe. Spanning the entire history of the Navaho people over the millennia seems a bit
much for the fourth grade; to the mother, it is plain that a report
will differ enormously according to whether one is looking at the
15th century, the 19th century, or last month.

The boy does not know. The teacher has not said. So mother
calls teacher to inquire about this elementary but—she thinks—
fundamental feature of the class assignment. What historical period does the teacher have in mind?

The teacher, it emerges, not only has no answer, she does not
think the question appropriate. The report, she says, is intended
to be about Indians, not about any particular time period. "We
teach the process method," she explains.

This is what E.D. Hirsch, the author of last year's best-selling
Cultural Literacy, calls "educational formalism." According to this
way of viewing the learning enterprise, it is not the knowledge entering one's head but the act of thinking that matters. So long as
one can analyze, it is not important what is being analyzed. Knowing how to read is important, but what one reads is not. In general, it is not the role of educators to tell youngsters what they
should know. It is their solemn obligation to help them "think
critically."

This emphasis on intellectual skills—"higher-order cognitive
skills" is today's term of art—eases all sorts of pedagogical dilem-
mas. "Thinking critically" avoids the relativist's agony of having
to designate "right" and "wrong" answers. It skirts those endless
disputes about "canons" and about "what knowledge is of greatest
value," the kind of thing that can tie up a faculty committee for
months. It sidesteps the clash between supporters of a common

culture and partisans of cultural pluralism (while awarding sure victory to the pluralists, since no common culture consists wholly of "reasoning skills"). It helps educators deal with the thorny issue of "values"—a term which, when used by the education establishment, signifies something one examines and at times "clarifies" rather than something one absorbs from elders, spiritual leaders, or teachers.

How to teach "higher-order cognitive skills" is the stuff of hundreds of education workshops and "in-service days" every month. Yet for all its trendiness, the notion is also of a piece with the long-prevailing philosophy of education schools and journals. This is the philosophy of progressive education, according to which the role of the teacher is not to dominate but to facilitate, and thinking creatively, being imaginative, and solving problems are preferable to following rules, internalizing traditions, and assimilating knowledge.

This strand of thought has wound through American education for a good part of the century, and by now has assumed the status of an orthodoxy. As one might expect, it is not without an implicit and sometimes explicit political component. Consider, for example, the enraged response of the education community to Hirsch's *Cultural Literacy*, a deeply liberal treatise which argues that disadvantaged and minority youngsters, and those from tattered families and bad neighborhoods, are ill-served by schools which fail to equip all their students with the essential background information needed for success in modern society. This work has been dismissed as elitist, as culturally hidebound, as an arid "list of facts," as the ravings of a latter-day Gradgrind, as a handbook to the game of *Trivial Pursuit*, as a plea for "rote learning," and as a harsh rejection of individual differences and ethnic diversity. Hirsch also stands accused of the crime of nationalism—as in, "He perpetuates the nation-state as the world's most fundamental political unit" (Catherine R. Stimpson, dean of the graduate school at Rutgers).

Thus do contemporary politics enter the educational debate, often clad in progressive pedagogical garb. One might have supposed facts to be ideologically inert, elements that all might agree on even while battling furiously over explanations and interpretations. But that is not true of American education today. My colleague Diane Ravitch and I have often cited with concern the astonishing finding that only a third of the eleventh-grade students surveyed for our 1987 book *What Do Our Seventeen-Year-Olds Know?* could place the Civil War in the correct half-century. Yet here is how Professor Stimpson dismisses that concern: "We would be more literate if at least two-thirds of those kids could pit the tail of time more accurately on the donkey of war." And here is former Weatherman William Ayers—a professor of, needless to say, education—on our book:

They are not interested in teaching as an activity that empowers the young to ask their own questions and seek their own answers. They are not concerned with teaching for self-determination, teaching for invention, teaching for transformation. They are not interested in teaching as a dialectical interplay of content and experience, past and present.

The curricular effects of "teaching for invention, teaching for transformation" have not changed much over the decades. My mother, for instance, attended a progressive school on the campus of Ohio State University in the mid-1930's. Here is how she once described it in a letter:

We had no exams, no report cards, and no training in English grammar. We were taught to "write as we feel" and to write naturally. We had no specific history classes, but a sort of hodgepodge amalgam of sociology, civics, history combined. We concentrated on different periods of history, but never did achieve a consecutive chronology of events . . . all of which left me with only a vague notion of history.

Half a century ago, there was still a price to be paid for ignorance: the college my mother wanted to attend informed her she was inadequately prepared, and would first have to go somewhere else and accumulate "some grades they could examine." Today, it is unlikely that any college in the land would signal directly that one's prior education was flawed—and even less likely that a paucity of English grammar or historical chronology would be deemed evidence of a problem grave enough to inconvenience a student displaying it.

And where English and history have led the way, mathematics and science, once regarded as the solidest parts of the school curriculum, are today not far behind. Here, too, we are now being told, there are no right answers. Here, too, the role of educators is to help students seek their own path.

In math education, among today's avant-garde the rage is for "problem solving," usually with the help of electronic calculators. "Drill and practice" are deemed archaic, and computation—those long rows of fractions to multiply and six-digit numbers to divide—is thought tiresome, hence dispensable. Nor is precision highly valued: getting the "right answer" is less important than devising a "creative" strategy for attacking the problem.

This is the view of the National Council of Teachers of Mathematics, which in March laid before the nation a whole new approach to math education. It is a view shared by the National Academy of Sciences, which has just published its own glossy tome entitled "Everybody Counts: A Report to the Nation on the Future of Mathematics Education." The panel that assembled it reads like a who's who of American education. Financial support came from four private foundations and five federal agencies. Here is a representative passage:

Unfortunately, as children become socialized by school and society, they begin to view mathematics as a rigid system of externally dictated rules governed by standards of accuracy, speed, and memory. . . . A mathematics curriculum that emphasizes computation and rules is like a writing curriculum that emphasizes grammar and spelling: both put the cart before the horse. . . . Teachers . . . almost always present mathematics as an established doctrine to be learned just as it was taught. This "broadcast" metaphor for learning leads students to expect that mathematics is about right answers rather than about clear creative thinking. . . .

One wonders how many of Jaime Escalante's poor Hispanic students in East Los Angeles would pass Advanced Placement calculus if their teacher scored "standards of accuracy, speed, and memory"—or how many middle-class adults could hope to balance their own checkbooks.

As for science, millions of dollars are now being spent in a highly publicized effort by the American Association for the Advancement of Science (AAAS) and its allies to revamp the nation's entire educational approach to the subject. The plan differs in two large ways from customary approaches. In the words of the panel:

One difference is that boundaries between traditional subject-matter categories are softened and connections are emphasized. . . .
A second difference is that the amount of detail that students are expected to retain is considerably less than in traditional science, mathematics, and technology courses. Ideas and thinking skills are emphasized at the expense of specialized vocabulary and memorized procedures. . . .

And here are some of the classroom precepts for teachers as set forth in the AAAS report: "do not separate knowing from finding out"; "deemphasize the memorization of technical vocabulary"; "use a team approach"; "reward creativity"; "encourage a spirit of healthy questioning"; "avoid dogmatism"; "promote aesthetic responses"; "emphasize group learning"; "counteract learning anxieties."

This is not advice for teaching cooking, or even sociology. Nor are these the words of an eccentric fringe. This broadside emanates from a panel cochaired by the former head of Bell Labs and the dean of undergraduate instruction of MIT, and including, besides the ubiquitous Albert Shanker, the former editor of *Scientific American* and the distinguished Harvard statistician Frederick Mosteller. The advice of this elevated group would certainly have fallen on friendly ears in my mother's progressive school of the 1930's. That it is being proffered in 1989 as a solution to our educational problems is, to say the least, remarkable—so remarkable that even the editors of the Washington *Post* were compelled to ask a simple question:

It's all very interesting, but will it do anything to address the much-documented inability of American students to answer international test questions on which way a plant will turn in the presence of sunlight? Not a thing. . . .

Indeed, nothing we have learned about education, past or present, at home or abroad, gives us any grounds for believing that the "process method," however elegantly refined, will ever produce people who know anything. This may seem a minor defect to educators, for whom specific knowledge is an unfashionable commodity. But it is also, finally, the reason why civilian control of education remains absolutely essential. We do not allow soldiers free rein with the "shooting method," doctors with the "surgery method," or bus drivers with the "honking method." Experts have their place. They also have their interests, and their severe limitations as shapers of policy. Left to follow their own norms, professional educators and their kindred organizations and think tanks will not just preserve the legacy of progressivism, they will enshrine the "process method" in larger, and emptier, cathedrals than ever before imagined.

Most Americans, when asked, say they want their children to know more than they do, and are appalled by the prospect that the next generation will know less. Yet so long as today's professional norms and beliefs hold sway, so long as they shape what actually occurs in the classroom, that is precisely the future that awaits our children. Changing the culture of any large enterprise is far more difficult than altering the specific policies by which it operates. But that is the central task confronting us—and also, one might add, confronting the man who would be our "education President."

HOW WASHINGTON CAN PITCH IN[6]

By the year 2000, every child must start school ready to learn.

The United States must increase the high school graduation rate to no less than 90%.

In critical subjects, at the fourth, eighth, and 12th grades, we must assess our students' performance.

U.S. students must be the first in the world in math and science achievement.

Every American adult must be a skilled, literate worker and citizen.

Every school must offer the kind of disciplined environment that makes it possible for our kids to learn.

And every school must be drug free.

—President George Bush in
"The State of the Union," January 31, 1990

Great Goals, Mr. President. Now it's time for you and the governors to get to work. By most measures the nation's education system is badly broken. Despite a doubling of spending in the 1980s, standardized test scores remain low, below those of our leading competitors. "We can't fix the system," says American Federation of Teachers President Albert Shanker with painful honesty. "We need radical change."

Nearly everyone agrees that states must take the lead. The Constitution omits any reference to education among federal powers, so the responsibility lies by implication with them. Along with local governments, states pay 86% of America's education bill. Moreover, the statehouse is closer to the problems—and the solutions. Says South Carolina Governor Carroll Campbell Jr.,

[6]Reprint of an article by Ann Reilly Dowd, *Fortune* staff writer. *Fortune* Sp. '90. 121: 53-5, 58, 62. Copyright © 1990 by *Fortune*. Reprinted with permission.

co-chairman of the National Governors' Association Education Task Force: "Communities need flexibility in dealing with their particular areas. Parents don't want the federal government running education."

Still, the President can focus public attention on the need for educational reform. George Bush already has earned an A for rhetoric by proclaiming goals, convening the first government-sponsored education summit, and honoring a teacher of the year. But to be worthy of the title Education President, he also needs to muster the resources of the executive branch to achieve results. On that score, he gets an Incomplete.

A President wise in the ways of Washington and committed to education reform would appoint a more dynamic Education Secretary than Lauro Cavazos, the first Hispanic president of Texas Tech University, who seems to have been picked more for ethnic balance than for his reformist zeal [Cavazos resigned and was replaced in March of 1991 by Lamar Alexander]. Such a President would create a new Cabinet Council on Human Resource Development that pulled together the Secretaries of Education, Labor, Health and Human Services, Agriculture, and Treasury, plus the Budget Director, for an all-out drive toward educational excellence. He would also appoint a high-level adviser in the White House to push important initiatives through political roadblocks. But Bush has done none of these things. Says former Labor Secretary Ann McLaughlin: "Managing U.S.-Soviet relations alone won't keep America strong. We need a national commitment to lifelong learning."

Though Bush has shown no interest in major increases in federal spending to improve education, he should. An epidemic of social ills from drug abuse to homelessness continues to distract youngsters from the business of learning. Washington must attack these problems more aggressively and improve the delivery of social services to the needy. One way is to tie federal aid to states to the development of so-called one-stop service centers in or near schools where poor people can get food stamps, housing, job training, and other kinds of help all in one place.

The single most important thing President Bush can do is push for more money for existing federal programs that prepare poor children for school. The highly effective Head Start preschool program, for instance, reaches about a fifth of the poor children eligible for it. But the Head Start budget should plan for higher teacher salaries and better quality control—not just more students.

Washington should also spend more on programs that provide nutrition and health care for needy children. A good example is recent federal legislation financing comprehensive social service centers along the lines of Chicago's innovative Beethoven Project. Funded from public and private sources, Beethoven trains older women in public housing developments to visit expectant mothers and tell them about available prenatal care, family counseling, and other social services. The program also provides health care, nutrition, and preschool classes for neighborhood children.

The payoffs from such investments are enormous both for individuals and for society. The House Select Committee on Children, Youth, and Families reports that a dollar invested in prenatal care saves up to $3 in hospital costs alone. A dollar invested in preschool education saves as much as $6 in special education, welfare, crime, and lost productivity. Says Ernest Boyer, president of the Carnegie Foundation for the Advancement of Teaching: "Early intervention is powerfully in America's self-interest."

The Administration can use its regulatory muscle as an instrument of change. Federal aid to education is so narrowly structured that it can penalize performance. For instance, computers bought with "Chapter 1" money for educationally disadvantaged children cannot be used at night to teach adults to read. And if a school succeeds in keeping more students from dropping out or failing, aid is reduced. The National Center on Education and the Economy, chaired by Apple Computer CEO John Sculley, has a sensible alternative: Allow states greater flexibility in the use of federal funds in exchange for adopting—and living by—ambitious student performance goals. Legislation along those lines introduced by Vermont Congressman Peter Smith deserves serious attention by Congress.

The federal government should play a more extensive role in educational research and development. While the Department of Education has established some measures of student achievement nationally, including the data below, it lacks the budget and in many cases the legal authority to gather information needed to compare countries, states, school districts, schools, or individual students. Education administrators, testing companies, and the Parent-Teacher Association—representing mostly teachers— have objected vehemently to some of the small steps Congress has taken to increase federal oversight. Educators object on grounds that accurate measures are not possible. But critics think they're mainly worried that comparisons will show how badly they're doing.

Some states are developing their own new measurements, but a coordinated approach demands federal leadership. A good beginning is New Mexico Senator Jeff Bingaman's national report card bill, which would set up a commission of experts to assess progress toward national goals, identify gaps in existing data, and make recommendations for improved testing.

Finally, Washington can spur innovation through well-designed pilot projects. The President has focused on the worthy goal of better teaching. His proposals include merit pay for excellent teachers and grants to states to improve math and science teaching and to develop alternative certification procedures.

But he has missed one enormous opportunity: the chance to lead the way to the classroom of the future by underwriting the development of interactive video software and training teachers in its use. Says California school superintendent Bill Honig, who has developed a new history video program with Lucasfilm, Apple Computer, and National Geographic: "Such investments can pay huge dividends."

Many governors have been pushing reform long enough to understand what works and what doesn't. Strategies are beginning to change. Most early efforts focused on tough rules: tighter course requirements, higher teacher certification standards, and the like. But performance did not improve markedly. Now many states are concentrating on results. Says Chester Finn, assistant secretary of education in the Reagan Administration: "The shift from regulating means to regulating ends represents a historic change."

The first state to move wholeheartedly in that direction was California. In 1983 the state's Democratic leaders launched a major drive to prepare youngsters for the new information-age job market and to function as citizens of a democracy. The goal-setting process involved educators, parents, community leaders, business, and labor. The state-financed program involved heavy investment in new technology and teacher development, and resulted in major changes in curriculum, textbooks, teaching methods, and testing. Schools were encouraged to seek waivers from any state regulations they felt got in the way of specific programs. The result: Despite a surge in enrollments—including many poor and bilingual children—eighth-graders' performance improved 25% in three years.

South Carolina followed a similar course with equally impressive results. In six years the state raised average scores on the Scholastic Aptitude Test 40 points, more than any other state. Fifteen other states have enacted such reforms, including Kentucky, which was forced to do so by the Kentucky Supreme Court. Because of the way Kentucky's schools were funded, among other problems, the court ruled that the whole system violated the state's constitution. Starting from scratch, the state has opted for a performance-based system that gives unprecedented freedom and responsibility to individual schools.

What lessons can be drawn from these pioneering efforts? First, successful reform requires cooperation among traditionally combative power centers. Responsibility must flow from the statehouse to the schoolhouse without loss of accountability. Business must get involved. School administrators and union leaders must share control with teachers, parents, and students.

It isn't easy. Says New Mexico Governor Garrey E. Carruthers, a Republican who just maneuvered a sweeping reform package through his Democratic legislature: "Make no mistake, it takes political leverage, good old-fashioned horse trading, and more money." To win support, Carruthers had to raise teachers' and administrators' salaries, fund after-school programs, and offer extra money to schools that restructured. The cost: $50 million a year more in revenues, raised through a 0.25% increase in gross-receipts taxes. His fellow Republicans howled, but the governor finally persuaded them with stiff accountability standards embedded in a report card bill. All 88 school districts must now report annually on how well their students do. Says Carruthers: "The key was accountability."

Many reform governors have found that accountability demands new measures of performance. Across America, most public schools rely on multiple-choice tests that measure a student's retention of facts but not the analytical skills that will be needed in the future. Critics say standardized tests discriminate against minorities and distort classroom instruction by putting too much emphasis on memorization.

To refocus students and teachers on creative thinking and teamwork, several states are experimenting with new forms of testing. Vermont plans to test fourth- and eighth-graders in writing and math using three methods: a uniform test, a portfolio of work developed over the course of the year, and a single piece chosen by the student.

In 1991, Connecticut will launch a new math and science assessment of high school students involving tasks that may take student teams as long as a semester to complete. A sample assignment: design, carry out, and report on an experiment to determine which food store in your community would save a family of four the most money over the course of a year.

Once standards are set, schools must be held to them. Minnesota, Nebraska, Iowa, Arkansas, and Ohio rely on consumers to provide discipline. In the most radical change in the history of U.S. public school education, these states allow parental choice—students can attend any public school in the state.

Eight other states intervene directly when schools don't make the grade. In the best systems the state first offers financial and managerial assistance. If that fails, the state takes over the school or shuts it down. One South Carolina elementary school was turned around when state officials introduced IBM's innovative Writing to Read computer program. In Jersey City, school administrators stuck with their methods even when the dropout rate topped 30%. Thomas Kean, who was then New Jersey's governor, threw out the recalcitrants and installed a new management team.

A way to win teachers' support is to free them of the regulatory strings that bind them like Gulliver lying on the beach. State boards of education often dictate what teachers teach and from what texts. States also control pay. Excellence is rarely rewarded: Pay is generally based on years served—or in some cases endured. Many teachers lack career ladders: a 30-year veteran does the same work as a new recruit.

Connecticut put teacher excellence at the center of its restructuring plan. The state has raised pay most 40% since 1986 to an average $37,339, and increased standards. New teachers serve under experienced mentors. Veterans have to take 90 hours of professional development every five years, at state expense.

New Jersey eliminated its shortage of quality teachers through an alternative certification process launched by Kean. Applicants without traditional education degrees have to pass a test and agree to a year of supervision and after-hours training. Says Kean: "It means engineers from Bell Labs can teach computer science, jazz musicians can teach music, and former private-school teachers can work in the public schools. The profession is revitalized, and there's a great big teacher surplus." Twenty-seven states are following New Jersey's lead.

A number of states are also experimenting with financial incentives. Eight offer teachers and schools financial rewards for outstanding performance. In South Carolina the money can be used to buy instructional materials and computers or to train teachers. Last year 265 of the state's 1,100 schools won over $4 million in incentive money.

States also must be greater fiscal equalizers among school districts. The Congressional Research Service reports that during the 1986–87 school year, over half the states spent twice as much per pupil in some school districts as in others; a third spent three times; New York, eight times. The courts have already required ten states to implement more equitable financing formulas, and lawsuits have been filed in ten others.

Another key is higher student expectations and opportunities. That's what Minnesota Governor Rudy Perpich learned from his pioneering program that gives 11th- and 12th-graders a state stipend to attend classes at state colleges and universities. Says Perpich, who also started the nation's first statewide choice program: "A number of students drop out because they are bored. Of all our reforms, this one is doing the most for education."

Louisiana Governor Buddy Roemer learned the same lesson from a generous oilman. Two years ago Patrick F. Taylor offered to pay college tuition for 180 poor seventh- and eighth-graders— most of whom had repeated two or more grades—if they stayed out of trouble and graduated from high school with a B average. Today 150 are still in high school (19 moved, 11 were dismissed). On the precollege ACT test, half the tenth-graders scored at least

18, close to the national average. Inspired by Taylor's kids, Roemer pushed a bill through the legislature that puts state money behind a similar statewide program.

Still, all the opportunities in the world may not be enough to help the student whose family life is abusive, who sleeps on the street, or who is addicted to drugs or alcohol. This is not a negligible number: New York City School Chancellor Joseph A. Fernandez says 28 babies a day are born to drug-addicted mothers, the equivalent of 365 kindergarten classes a year. Schools are not equipped to solve such problems. But to succeed in their mission, they will increasingly have to help students and their families get the help they need. xxxxxx

In Albuquerque, New Mexico, the New Futures School is tackling the problem of teenage pregnancy. Founded by volunteers 20 years ago in the basement of a YWCA, New Futures combines on-site health and child care, nutrition advice, personalized counseling, and job placement for 500 young women a year. While more than half of teen mothers nationwide drop out, about 75% of those in the New Futures program graduate and go on to jobs or higher education. Honeywell Chairman James Reiner was so impressed that he flew two planeloads of Minneapolis-St. Paul city leaders to Albuquerque to see the school firsthand. Convinced, they are now trying to build their own New Futures schools.

Who will pay for such promising reforms? Ideally, all levels of government. But given Bush's no-new-taxes posture, the reality is that state and local governments will have to pick up the check for most of them. That's not necessarily bad. Many governors, like Carruthers, have had the courage to raise taxes. And if New Mexico is a bellwether, voters have grasped a truth that still escapes many politicians: Either America pays now for educational excellence, or it pays more, much more, later.

II. THE CURRICULUM DEBATE: MULTICULTURALISM

EDITOR'S INTRODUCTION

Partly because of immigration, large ethnographic changes have occurred in the U.S. within the last decade. It is estimated, for example, that by the year 2000, one in three people living in New York State will be a member of a minority group. Accordingly, a consciousness of and respect for cultural diversity has been given a high priority in the school curriculum in the 1990s. An approach to education that affirms the value of cultural minorities, will surely play an increasingly important role in the schools in the future. Multicultural programs, however, will have to be wisely planned if conflict is to be avoided.

In New York State, multiculturalism has attracted attention particularly since Education Commissioner Thomas Sobol asked a 24-member task force to undertake a study of the curricular materials developed by the State Education Department for its elementary and secondary schools. In July 1989, the group, the Task Force on Minorities: Equity and Excellence, issued its report, "A Curriculum of Inclusion." Presently under consideration by the State Board of Regents, the report argues that a sweeping overhaul of the curriculum is needed to counteract entrenched stereotyping and denigration of minorities, which have had a "terribly damaging effect on the psyches of young people of African, Asian, Latino, and Native American descent."

Excerpts from the report, containing general statements from main section, appear as the first selection in this section. What the report says in essence is that it is not enough to give enlarged coverage to minority cultures. These cultures must be presented as being equal in authority to the dominant white European one. An analogy is used in which a long table at which the European culture is at the head is replaced by a round table providing equitable treatment for all cultures. Criticism of "A Curriculum of Inclusion" was not long in coming. In the second selection, represented from *The New Republic*, Scott McConnell and Eric Breindel attack the report sharply, noting that its often strident tone and phraseology suggested a "Third World-style radical political perspective."

In the next article, Lawrence Auster writing in the *National Review* characterizes "A Curriculum of Inclusion" as a "poorly thought-out document, steeped in racial victimology and hostility to the West," which seeks to dismantle the dominant culture. In a lengthier article from the *American Scholar*, Diane Ravitch distinguishes between pluralistic multiculturalism and the new particularistic one embodied in the report, which would keep cultural groups separate and at odds. "Particularism has its intellectual roots," Ravitch writes, "in the ideology of ethnic separatism," and would turn the school curriculum into a battle field in which ethnic groups contend for what gets taught.

Finally, in a speech delivered to the Conference on Workforce Diversity and Economic Competitiveness, Don Blandin, the director of the Business-Higher Education Forum of the American Council on Education discusses the changing ethnic and racial makeup of American society. Citing recent trends in immigration and ever increasing minority populations, Blandin posits that education is the only hope for drawing "minorities into the economic mainstream."

A CURRICULUM OF INCLUSION[1]

I. INTRODUCTION

Society has given the educational system responsibility for reducing ignorance, one of the root causes of negative stereotyping and its attendant destructive behavior. Unfortunately, stereotyping and misinformation have become institutionalized and have become part of the dominant culture enveloping everyone.

African Americans, Asian Americans, Puerto Ricans/Latinos, and Native Americans have all been the victims of a cultural oppression and stereotyping that has characterized institutions—including the educational institutions—of the United

---

[1]Excerpts from "Task Force on Minorities: Equity and Excellence. A Curriculum of Inclusion." A report by the Task Force on Minorities, to Thomas Sobol, New York State Education Commissioner. Pgs. 6–42. Copyright © 1989 by the New York State Education Department. Reprinted by permission.

States and the European American world for centuries. In its most extreme form, the stereotyping of African peoples and African Americans through the "Tarzan syndrome" and the "Amos and Andy syndrome" has a parallel for Asian Americans through "Charlie Chan," for Latinos through "Frito Bandito," and for Native Americans through "The Lone Ranger and Tonto." This negative characterization and stereotyping is still found in books, films, advertisements, television programs, and school systems. The negative characterizations have a terribly damaging effect on the psyche of young people of African, Asian, Latino, and Native American descent, and an equally damaging, though different, effect on young people of European [American] descent.

These characterizations have contributed to intellectual victimization and miseducation of Americans of all cultures: members of minority cultures are alienated and devalued, members of the majority culture are exclusionary and over-valued. Because of the depth of the problem and the tenacity of its hold on the mind, only the most stringent measures can have significant impact. Change in this area is imperative so that intellectual honesty and bias-free education can replace miseducation. Then the educational system will encourage the development of positive self-esteem and self-management skills needed in all young people in a pluralistic society.

In recent years the New York State Education Department has developed curricular materials whose goal was to recognize the pluralism of United States culture and end the "cultural elitism" of the past. Continuing problems of high dropout rates, poor academic performance, and ethnic friction in our schools and in our society at large have called into question whether the goals of curricular change have been met. Responding to a request by New York State Education Commissioner Thomas Sobol, the Task Force on Minorities: Equity and Excellence undertook a study of the curricular materials developed by the State Education Department for elementary and secondary schools of New York State. The Task Force accepted as appropriate a goal of New York's education system as stated by the Regents of the University of the State of New York, that

Each student will develop the ability to understand, respect, and accept people of different races; sex; cultural heritage; national origin; religion; and political, economic, and social background, and their values, beliefs, and attitudes.

The study by the Task Force sought to determine the extent to which curricular materials prepared and distributed by the State Education Department do indeed support that goal. To the extent that materials deliberately or inadvertently lead students to misunderstand, to disrespect, or to reject people who are different from themselves, the will of the Regents is being thwarted. The Task Force members believe that understanding, respect, self-acceptance, and acceptance of others who are different from oneself are the sine qua non of a vibrant, dynamic, economically and socially healthy state which is capable not only of sustaining itself but also of providing leadership to the rest of the nation into the 21st Century.

For more than three hundred years, New York has been home to diverse peoples from all regions of the earth. Native Americans were here to welcome new settlers from Holland, Senegal, England, Indonesia, France, the Congo, Italy, China, Iberia— from everywhere. Today, representatives of perhaps every known culture and background can be found living in New York. Members of each culture have contributed to the greatness of the Empire State, and to its problems. And as each new generation of young people moves through the school system, the curriculum must help each child "learn knowledge, skills, and attitudes which enable development of self esteem" as well as help each child "understand, respect, and accept" as being inherently equal those who are different: those who look different or dress differently, those who believe or live differently, and those who talk or pray differently.

The goal of the Task Force was formidable. Thousands of pages of curricular materials, in nearly one hundred discrete curriculum guides, were reviewed "to determine whether individually or collectively the materials adequately and accurately reflect the pluralistic nature of our society." The study focused on Native American, Latino, Asian American, and African American cultures, four major cultural groupings which historically have been excluded from the dominant perspective (European American) of [the] New York State. There are many other cultures in New York besides these four, but our time and resources were limited. Indeed, it should be emphasized at this point that there is great cultural diversity within all of the cultural groups referred to in the report, and care must be taken to recognize and respect the variations. The Task Force firmly believes that the manner in which the European American culture has interacted with these four general cultural groupings is basically similar to the way it has interacted with all other cultures. Any actions taken to make accurate and open the relationships between these five cultures, their histories and achievements, will be applicable to interactions between these cultures and all other cultures not specifically addressed in this report.

II. METHODOLOGY

The Task Force divided itself into five sub-committees based on curricular disciplines (social studies, math and science, English and literature, art and music, and second languages). Members of each sub-committee reviewed all materials appropriate to its topic.

To bring greater specific expertise to the study, the Task Force retained four curricular experts to conduct an exhaustive review of the material. Each consultant was required to review all materials to determine whether they "reflect the pluralistic nature of our society." The appropriateness of the curricula relative to each of the four target cultures was studied by a curriculm expert from that culture. The consultants were further required to identify any materials that "do not adequately and accurately reflect pluralism, and to explain how they are lacking." On the positive side, the consultants were to identify "any materials that are particularly strong in reflecting pluralism and explain how they accomplish their inclusiveness." . . .

Task Force members, drawing on their own wealth of experience and expertise, recognized that many materials prepared by a dominant culture to portray members of or events in another culture could be biased. The bias would be a tendency to include people and activities considered to be supportive of the dominant culture and to exclude people and activities considered threatening, distasteful, or embarrassing. Thus, the consultants were required to review all curricular materials to determine whether prominent members of all cultures "are presented in full dimension as opposed to being presented in such a way that only those aspects of their lives more or less readily acceptable to the dominant culture are apparent." . . .

All curricular materials were evaluated, with each of the reviewers concentrating on social studies as the pivotal curricular area. While each reviewer felt that mathematics and science do not lend themselves as well to multicultural treatment because of their technical nature, there was consensus that no topic is truly culture-free and that by ostensibly omitting cultural references from science and mathematics materials, a subtle message is given to all children that all science and mathematics originated within the European culture. Thus, there is a clear need to include in the science and mathemmatics curricular materials references to the many contributions made by people from a variety of cultures.

While clearly much was found lacking in currently used materials, some excellent material is being used. Indeed, each evaluator mentioned particular strengths and positive aspects of some of the curricular materials. Nevertheless, after the analysis of how different cultural/ethnic experiences are treated in the state-wide curricular materials, the consultants (in spite of minor differences of approach to the study) came to the inescapable conclusion that the materials do not "individually or collectively adequately and accurately reflect the pluralistic nature of society in the United States." For the most part, the development of the United States is depicted from the dominant monocultural view of being a preserve of European Americans, or specifically the Anglo-Saxons, and their values. The various contributions of the African Americans, the Asian Americans, the Puerto Ricans/ Latinos, and the Native Americans have been systematically distorted, marginalized, or omitted. Although the special syllabi relating to multicultural ethnic group experiences are an improvement over former materials, they are peripheral to the main sweep of the education process. They represent only a beginning, underscoring how much more has to be done.

III. EXCLUSIONARY TENDENCIES IN CURRENT CURRICULAR MATERIALS

*   *   *   *   *

B. Endemic Omissions from the Current Curriculum

It is clear from the materials presented for review and analysis that a considerable effort has been made over the past few years by the State Education Department to revise curricula to reflect the multicultural nature of American society. Some of these revisions represent substantial progress, particularly in the Social

Studies area. Unfortunately, many of the recent curricular revisions represent change in form and not in substance. In view of the need to prepare young people for the challenges of the 21st Century, which will center, in part, around the reality of changing demographics, more substantive revision must be done. People from cultures now largely omitted from the curriculum already comprise a majority of the world's population and will in the not-so-distant future constitute a majority of New York's population.

Although individually, several syllabido represent substantial progress in portraying the multicultural nature of American society, in general, the curricular materials do not adequately and accurately reflect cultural experience in America. This is because revision to date cannot counteract deeply rooted racist traditions in American culture. Merely adding marginal examples of "other" cultures to an assumed dominant culture cannot reverse long established and entrenched policies and practices of that dominant culture. Much more extensive corrective action beyond recent revisions is needed to create the dynamics of positive change and to encourage attitudes toward differences as being "equal to" rather than "less than."

$$* \quad * \quad * \quad * \quad *$$

C. Weaknesses in the Social Studies and Ethnic Studies Curriclum

1. General Shortcomings

One of the major goals outlined by the Board of Regents for elementary and secondary education in New York State is that "Each student will develop the ability to understand, respect and accept people of different races; sex; cultural heritage; national origin; religion; and political, economic and social background, and their values, beliefs and attitudes." It also states that "Each student will learn knowledge, skills and attitudes which enable development of self-esteem, as well as the ability to maintain physical, mental and emotional health," while "understanding the ill effects of alcohol, tobacco and other drugs." These statements and others represent a laudable attempt by the Board of Regents to include multicultural goals and objectives in their overall plan of action for New York elementary and secondary education. This framework provides the basis for development of revised curricular material, particularly in the area of social studies. . . .

The crucial factor of implementation at the local level and in the classroom calls into question the efficacy even those syllabi that seriously attempt to include multi-cultural perspectives. Another major weakness (which has already been mentioned in this report) is that much of curricular material which has been produced presents the *form* of multiculturalism but not the *substance*.

An example of multicultural form but lack of substance can be found in the *Social Studies 1 (1987) Syllabus*. On the cover is a multicultural collection of families, which is appropriate because the focus in the initial education level is on social interaction and family relations. The images presented are a European American family, an Asian American family, and an African American family. This is multiculturalism, at least in form. Upon a closer look, it is clear that multicultural substance has been omitted. First, the European American family is represented by three generations, the African American family includes just a single parent. A subtle message is thereby conveyed about differences in family structure in different cultures. Second, since every illustration should not and cannot include representatives of all cultural groups, the fact that neither a Latino family nor a Native American family included is not in and of itself a weakness. However, nowhere in the syllabus is there another illustration featuring a Latino or Native American. When some people in a society become invisible, the excluded people de-value their self-worth and the included people over-value their self-worth.

These two weaknesses are cited as examples of Eurocentric multiculturalism. It reflects a larger problem found in most of the materials, namely, that multiculturalism developed in the syllabi is additive and not at the center of the endeavors. It involves form and not substance and projects dominant European American values.

The overall impression of the Task Force is that there has been an attempt to broaden content to reflect the pluralism of American society without changing the traditional approach. The European American monocultural perspective prevails. Its value system and norms dominate, while the contributions of African Americans, Asian Americans, Native Americans, and Puerto Ricans/Latinos and their experiences are extremely ambiguous and marginalized. Very few individuals other than European Americans emerge from the outlines and assume a meaningful place in history. Rarely is one of the basic themes truly related to the multicultural American experience. Even the suggested activities for learners and teachers omit or limit those projects that would make the understanding of pluralism more realistic. . . .

Shortcomings such as those cited above are found throughout the curricular materials. Major problems are evident in terms of the presentation of multicultural images, the frequency of appearances, and their strategic place. As a result, when the materials were viewed from the point of view of contextual relevancy and visibility, most were found to reflect pluralism inadequately and inaccurately.

*   *   *   *   *

V. AN ALTERNATIVE CONCEPTUAL APPROACH

A. The Rationale

Although the reviewed curricular materials reflect a serious attempt to enlighten the population and even include pluralism, there appears to be a reluctance to include content and key issues concerning African American, Asian American, Latino, and Native American peoples in an integrated, substantive fashion. This is very unfortunate in view of the recently developed evidence documenting the significant role that Africa, Asia, and Latin America have played in world history. We expect the school experience to expand the scope of knowledge of our youth and to develop their natural reflective and critical capacities. Instead, the monocultural perspective of traditional American education restricts the scope of knowledge. It acts as a constraint on the critical thinking of African American, Asian American, Native American, and Puerto Rican/Latino youth because of its hidden assumptions of "white supremacy" and "white nationalism."

The learning processes in our schools should stimulate and expand the intellectual quest for knowledge; all too often the current approach "turns off" the child who is not European American. In the mind, this child only sees a negative reflection of self, family, community, and heritage because in the contemporary education experience "different" has generally been taught to mean "not as good as." As a result, instead of the learning process "turning students on," it produces the opposite effect, fostering low self-esteem and negative expectations. Many young people

leave the school system out of frustration and feelings of inadequacy or they are pushed out as non-achievers. On the other
hand, the near exclusion of other cultures in the curriculum gives
European American children the seriously distorted notion that
their culture is the only one to have contributed to the growth
of our society. Such distortion gives European American children
an inappropriate encouragement to disparage children of other
cultures.

The failure of the educational system to meet the needs of African American, Asian American, Latino, and Native American
youth, its limited ability to foster positive socialization processes
for children of these cultures, and its fostering an inappropriately
elitist attitude in European American children, makes it imperative to re-examine and re-evaluate the total educational experience. The educational system of New York State has a unique
opportunity to reduce ignorance and to reverse the negative experiences of youth by re-examining the specific ways in which its
mission is carried out and how it has been affected by both hidden
and intentional cultural bias.

This review of the K-12 curricula of The Board of Regents
of New York State confirms the need for major curricular revision. All four consultants agree: It is time for a change.

B. A MULTICULTURAL MODEL OF HISTORY

A new frame of reference is needed, through which students
and teachers both can effectively analyze the major events and issues concerning human development. An educational system
centered around the Eurocentric world view is limited and narrow and fails to provide a global perspective. Inevitably, it projects the Anglo-Saxon value system and prevents European
American youth, as well as youth of other cultures, from the benefit of a broad-based learning experience.

Simultaneously, the Eurocentric world view perpetuates processes of negative socialization for African Americans, Asian
Americans Latinos and Native Americans. Consequently, the education systems in New York State and throughout the United
States of America have produced processes of "miseducation"
that must be challenged and changed. These processes have
helped institutionalize systems of mediocrity and failure, particularly in the urban areas and among the rural poor. Recent reports
prepared for the Governor of the State of New York and the

Commissioner of Education have confirmed these shortcomings and failures of the education system.

The educational review of the curriculum revealed that even well prepared syllabi continue to promote and maintain this European American value system. As a result, the story of the United States of America and the State of New York has been centered around the Anglo-Saxon elite while the "Other America" has been rendered invisible or at best, marginal. Information about African Americans, Asian Americans, Latinos, and Native Americans is generally perceived as additive or supplemental even by many teachers who genuinely believe it is needed in the curriculum. Too few education professionals, however, are committed to make this information a focal point of teaching content, major ideas, and student activities.

The multicultural model poses a fundamental and enduring alternative to the existing academic curriculum and its exclusive, elitist ideological foundations. It challenges the education establishment and its various components to deal with previously ignored important areas of knowledge and human experience. These areas of knowledge, old and new, are either relegated to the periphery of what might be called the Eurocentric "elitist" traditional curriculum or they are completely omitted from the learning process. In the traditional Eurocentric educational program, we are presented with "white nationalism" that makes marginal all other peoples. An innovative and creative multicultural model moves experiences previously consigned to the margins to a large, central area. Here all cultural experiences can be the catalyst for a truly exciting, intellectually stimulating, and culturally invigorating learning process.

In the real world, we are confronted with the universal reality of cultural pluralism within New York State, the nation, and the world. Our educational curriculum must prepare all of our youth to operate in this reality.

C. A New Approach

Perhaps surprisingly, we can find an analogy to a new model of education in a revered legend of the very group that has largely been responsible for maintaining the monocultural model. King Arthur, in a brilliant and effective move to prevent an inappropriate hierarchy from developing amongst his nobles, created his Round Table. When all gathered, they sat in relative equality of opportunity to serve and show respect for each other. The multicultural model seats all cultures at a round table, each offering something to the collective good, each knowing and respecting others, and each gaining from the contribution of others. In contrast, the monocultural model has placed European culture at the head of a long, narrow table; at best, some other cultures are treated as invited guests sitting some distance from the head of the table; at worst, some cultures are not even invited to the table.

There are major problems with our current "head of the table, plus others" approach to education. The group taking the head of the table status comes to believe in its inherent superiority and that others are at the table through its beneficence. The others come to believe they are indeed inferior to the head group and act out an inferior role, glad to be invited to sit at [a] table with the head and make some minor contribution to the meal.

People of all cultures are thus currently given a distorted view of reality. European culture has no inherent claim to superiority, yet our educational system teaches European American children that their culture is the standard against which all other cultures are found wanting. African American, Asian American, Latino, Native American culture or any other culture has no inherent weakness. Our educational system, however, teaches children of these cultures that they are marginal, have contributed little of substance to the nation of their birth, and are fortunate that European Americans are so noble as to grant them limited access to the conditions of the dominant culture. From this distortion of reality grows racism, arrogance, and self-doubt.

The old curriculum is essentially based on the premise that America has one cultural heritage augmented by minor contributions from other peoples who by and large have presented "problems" to the primary culture. To combat teaching and learning based on this premise, a radical, new approach to building a curriculum is needed.

The search for truth and the pursuit of knowledge must be broad-based and not limited to one culture's experiences. It must be global and include the various cultures that come to us out of Africa, Asia, the Caribbean, and Latin America as well as out of Europe. Non-European peoples make up ninety percent of the world's population and have had an enormous impact on the development of the United States of America. Education should be designed to provide a truer picture of the growth of America and correct as many as possible of the false images, mis-information, and errors about the history and present reality of Americans.

A truly multicultural curriculum represents a body of knowledge about the African, Asian, Latin American/Caribbean, Native American, and European experience and presents an alternate approach to the education system. To the extent that this alternative curriculum with its equitable treatment of all cultures eliminates omissions, corrects erroneous material, provides new analyses, contradicts fallacious assumptions, and challenges ethnocentric traditions of all kinds—it improves existing educational endeavors and becomes the basis for innovative, creative models of learning for all students and staff.

VI. RECOMMENDATIONS

The Task Force believes that a multicultural curriculum must be developed and can be developed in the near future. The importance of the task to millions of New York State school children, who will provide the leadership and labor force for the state in the Twenty-first Century, is too great even to hesitate before moving swiftly toward revisions. To accomplish the critical work, the Task Force recommends:

1. That the Commissioner of Education give continuing vitality to his initiative for multicultural educational development by creating the position of Special Assistant to the Commissioner for Cultural Equity. This should be a staff position reporting directly to the Commissioner. Among the duties of the Special Assistant should be:

1.1 informing the Commissioner on a regular and continuing basis the degree of implementation of, and problems preventing full conformity with, policies and directives intended to ensure that all cultures receive equitable and accurate attention in the educational curriculum and members of all cultures experience excellence in the schools of New York State;

1.2 assisting Education Department staff in finding and utilizing the resources that are available to aid them in executing the Commissioner's policies and directives;

1.3 working with the office of the State Education Department charged by the Commissioner with identifying, analyzing, and resolving problems that arise anywhere in the educational system affecting the implementation of the multicultural program; and

1.4 Serving as an ombudsman to whom minority pupils, parents, and the public-at-large, and Education Department personnel can seek assistance for the satisfactory resolution of concerns regarding equity and excellence.

2. That the Commissioner direct appropriate staff to undertake without delay a revision of all curricula and curricular materials so as to ensure that they are compatible with goals of equity and excellence for all cultures within our society. A restructuring of the entire curriculum must be done not in a piecemeal fashion but rather in a fundamental manner to ensure that the pluralistic nature of our society is clearly represented and that students of all cultures are properly educated. Aspects of cooperation and amicability among all cultures should be stressed over conflict and violence.

3. That the Commissioner direct that all groups involved in the development, dissemination, and evaluation of curricula and curricular materials reflect in their own composition the multicultural diversity found in New York's schools.

4. That the Commissioner lead his staff to understand that the adequate, accurate presentation of multicultural diversity within curricular materials requires that the history, achievements, aspirations, and concerns of people of all cultures be equitably and accurately infused into and made an integral part of all curricula. Curricular materials must no longer be presented to teachers and to their pupils in a hierarchical form with some cultures as appendages to an assumed primary culture.

5. That the State Education Department begin intensive discussions with textbook publishers to encourage them to publish texts that are multicultural in substance. All changes made to reflect multicultural concerns in New York will also be valid throughout the rest of the nation.

6. That the Regents mandate new conditions of teacher and school administrator certification in the State of New York, to include appropriate education and competence in multicultural education. To accomplish this, personnel from the State Education Department should work with teacher education and education administration faculties to develop new curricula with a multicultural foundation in college and university education programs. Upon implementation of new standards in teacher and administrator programs, all state certifications of teachers, administrators, and college or university education programs must include multicultural competencies.

7. That the State Education Department find ways to encourage school districts to provide immediate, effective opportunities for current staffs to gain competence in multicultural education. The goal should be to improve staff performance and enhance staff understanding of multicultural behavior and education. School district effectiveness in achieving the goals of multicultural education should be assessed routinely through the existing Comprehensive Assessment Report.

8. That the State Education Department work with all school districts and colleges and universities to develop and implement effective recruitment programs to increase the number of cultures represented in their faculties and staffs. The increased cultural diversity of the faculties and staffs will impact positively on all students, lending overt support to the multicultural basis of the classroom instruction. Members of under-represented cultures can serve as role models for some students and examples for others and are likely to bring increased sensitivity to culturally diverse issues.

9. That the Commissioner of Education give this curriculum report the greatest possible attention and the widest possible circulation to key individuals in the State of New York, making the subject of planning "A Curriculum of Inclusion" a central one in the entire education community of the State.

HEAD TO COME[2]

Battles over what children will be taught in school always have an ideological aspect. Such struggles occur at every educational level from day care to graduate school, but the public school system, long a cockpit for political passions, is especially vulnerable. And those passions are never more engaged than when the fight involves social studies and history, because any picture of the past implies judgments about the nature of the present and the needs of the future.

[2]Reprint of an article by Scott McConnell, editorial board member of the New York *Post*, and Eric Breindel, editorial page editor, New York *Post*. *The New Republic*, Ja 8 & 15 '90. 202: 18, 20-1. Copyright © 1990 by *The New Republic*. Reprinted with permission.

A still obscure controversy in the education bureaucracy of New York state may herald the next stage of what has become a national school curriculum struggle. Last July selected New Yorkers—politicians, professional educators, and journalists—received an 80-page report titled "A Curriculum of Inclusion." The report was produced by a task force appointed by the state's Education Commissioner, Thomas Sobol, and chaired by Hazel Dukes, a widely respected New York political personality who serves as statewide chair of the NAACP. The 16 other members of the task force are either educators or activists concerned with minority affairs. Their report bluntly endorses a radical and deeply pessimistic critique of American society.

The task force's mission was to consider the New York state elementary and high school curriculum in light of the needs of blacks, Hispanics, and other minority students; to determine if the curriculum was insensitive or irrelevant to these needs; and, if appropriate, to propose changes. "A Curriculum of Inclusion" is the result. It raises the question of what vision of American society will inform what New York's schoolchildren will be taught. Should the schools emphasize that the multifarious cultural strands of American society coexist with and contribute to each other through citizenship in a polity that is open to all but is Western in its origins and major institutions? Or, as the task force recommends, should the education system stress the separate—often non-Western—ethnic identities of New York's students, while treating the society's main institutions as instruments of "European-American" domination?

The task force was convened to meet what both educators and employers regard as a growing problem: while non-whites should make up a growing percentage of New York's work force, "in almost every quantifiable measure of performance," according to the report itself, "large numbers of children of non-European descent are not doing as well as expected." This lack of success in school means that many will be unable to meet the entry-level requirements of New York's major corporate employers.

The Sobol report offers one main explanation for this phenomenon: it is the result of "stereotyping and misinformation"—which has "had a damaging effect on the psyche of young people of African, Asian, Latino, and Native American descent." Accordingly, while members of minority cultures come to feel "alienated and devalued [by what they are taught], members of the majority culture are exclusionary and overvalued."

The report's principal author is Harry Hamilton, a professor of atmospheric science at the State University of New York at Albany. Neither Hamilton nor the other members of the task force—as exemplified by Dukes, its chair—are known for their radical sensibilities. The responsibility for the Sobol report's often extremist tone, therefore, probably lies largely with the task force's chief consultant, Leonard Jeffries, chairman of the Department of Black Studies at the City College of New York, who is credited with helping create the initial draft.

The report's very first sentence illustrates that tone: "African Americans, Asian Americans, Puerto Ricans/Latinos, and Native Americans have all been the victims of an intellectual and educational oppression that has characterized the culture and institutions of the United States and the European American world for centuries." Here as elsewhere, the report is marked by a phraseology that suggests a Third World-style radical political perspective.

The task force's exhaustive review of New York's teaching materials turned up very little that even arguably documents its charge that existing curricular materials are marked by a "systematic bias" that reflects "hidden assumptions of 'white supremacy and white nationalism,'" and nothing at all that can properly be termed racist. The few concrete instances that are cited are trivial.

For example, the panel notes that a single text makes reference to the "Spanish-American War," thereby failing to conform to the new academic fashion, which is to designate that conflict as the "Spanish-Cuban-American War." Another complaint is the failure of a high school social studies unit on Africa to incorporate materials on Egypt and the Nile Valley. The result is that students are not taught that Africa was "the birthplace of humanity and earliest cradle of civilization." This "removal of Egypt and the Nile Valley from Africa," according to the report, "is a perfect example of the unwillingness or inability to move away from Eurocentric conceptualization and modality."

The report locates the roots of this ostensible bias in the way in which school texts emphasize the European origins of American culture and institutions. According to it, the curriculum "gives European-American children the seriously distorted notion that their culture is the only one to have contributed to the growth of our society." Among the various ways the report recommends that white students be stripped of their "inappropriately elitist attitudes" is to teach American history so that students learn that ours is a deeply flawed political system.

This approach is elaborated in Jeffries's appendix to the report, which evaluates the curriculum from the point of view of African American culture. While conceding that much of the material used in New York's schools "represents substantial progress in portraying the multicultural nature of American society," Jeffries nevertheless asserts flatly that the curriculum reflects "deep-seated pathologies of racial hatred."

"Action to root out this illness," Jeffries warns, "must be proactive and substantial in view of the generations of indoctrination and the strength of the processes of institutionalization." He adds: "It is too little too late to believe that inclusion of multicultural perspectives on the pluralism of American society can reverse long established and entrenched policies and practices. Much more severe corrective action is needed to create the dynamics of positive change."

The corrective action Jeffries has in mind is illustrated by his analysis of teaching materials pertaining to the American Revolution. He faults the curriculum for failing to present the Founders as slaveholders intent on "sacrificing higher ideals on the alter [sic] of materialism and profitmaking." In a section on the early history of the newly independent republic, Jeffries writes:

Under *Major Ideas*, the syllabus states that, "The United States Constitution was an advanced revolutionary plan of government in its time and remains so today." It further notes that "the Constitution represents the embodiment of the belief in human dignity, liberty, justice, and equality in theory, but not always in practice." Unfortunately, this type of "White Nationalism" or egocentrism blinds us as to the flawed nature of the processes, and the document and the subsequent political system that emerged and evolved through the years.

He goes on to describe "political parties, the President's Cabinet and committee system in Congress" as "effective vehicles for articulating and aggregating the interests of the rich and powerful, the true benefactor of the New Anglo-Saxon Model." He concludes, "Somehow or other, there is something vulgar and revolting in glorifying a process that heaped undeserved rewards on a segment of the population while oppressing the majority."

he proposal was released at the July meeting of the New
Board of Regents, the body that determines state education
. Professor Harry Hamilton, a member of the Commission-
ask Force on Minorities, which prepared the report, told
gents: "We're on the brink of something very important
w York and the nation. We have to change the entire
ork in the way we look at ourselves as a nation." Hamilton
mythic imagery: "Instead of one group, European Amer-
the head of a long table, with other cultures present only
d guests, we will have a Round Table with all cultures
itting at their own long table, the Regents received the
ith enthusiasm. Even conservatives liked it; former
r Willard Genrich, one of a tiny minority on the Board
ist tried to block a major expansion of bilingual educa-
ed: "This is an excellent document and we should pro-
."

nately, if their recent handling of bilingual education
the Regents seem likely to decide on the curriculum
asis of uplifting slogans about a new America rather
hought about the plan's contents. The report does
good ideas about widening the curriculum to reflect
riences; but on the whole it is a poorly thought-out
ped in racial victimology and hostility to the West.
Western-oriented education robs minority youth
"'turns off' the child who is not European
ot backed up by any evidence at all. When we re-
as W. E. B. Du Bois and Martin Luther King, as
other American blacks who were shining prod-
ered" education, it is hard to take that idea seri-
a group's curricular "invisibility" harms its self-
anese Americans done so well? Asians have
led to the litany of aggrieved and ego-damaged
usible the notion of a blanket educational op-
-whites and the resulting need for a radical

report concedes the presence of substantial
nt (as well as the absence of negative stereo-
curriculum. A series of textbook reviews
nority viewpoint shows that "there has been
roaden the content to reflect the pluralism
But such inclusion, says the report, does

The report also proposes, as a further solution to the problem
of "White Nationalism" in the curriculum, that more effort be
made to expose students to historical heroes from minority cultures. Some of its specific recommendations are astonishing. As
an appropriate Hispanic role model, for example, the Sobol team
suggests Pedro Albizu Campos, the Puerto Rican nationalist leader whose terrorist group tried to assassinate President Truman
in 1950 and shot up the House of Representatives in 1954.

Referring to "Eurocentrism," the report argues that due to
"the depth of the problem, only the most stringent measures can
have significant impact." Thus it calls for a wholesale revision of
textbooks and of the curriculum itself. This process would be
overseen by a new branch of the bureaucracy, the office of a
"Special Assistant to the Commissioner for Cultural Equity." The
mission of this office would be to ensure that "all cultures receive
equitable and accurate attention in the educational curriculum
and members of all cultures experience excellence in the schools
of New York State."

The extremist language of the Sobol group may ultimately
prove its undoing. But even if it had come up with a more judi-
ciously phrased document—one less eager to replace
"Eurocentrism" with a Third World view of the American experience and less eager to portray America's leaders as villains—it is
worth asking whether it is substantively wise for New York to
construct a curriculum that seeks to understate the impact of European thought and institutions on American history. It is wise,
moreover, to encourage minority students to feel that the mainstream language and culture of the United States does not belong
to them?

It is impossible to deny that America's basic political institutions were created by men steeped in European intellectual traditions. These traditions were essential to the establishment of
political democracy on these shores. And in the years since the
Founders, immigrants from all over the world have come here because they were attracted by that democracy and the vibrant
economy it engendered. This blend produced a genuinely pluralist society—indeed, the very concept of pluralism is itself a product of the European (or "Eurocentric") tradition.

It would be no tragedy, of course, for social studies courses
to include an examination of the political values of non-Western

traditions, as long as that didn't mean dropping Madison and Jefferson. But it seems silly to deny that many new Americans left regions of the world where other political traditions dominate precisely because these immigrants found non-Western institutions stultifying and oppressive. It is hard not to read the Sobol report—both in its specific recommendations and in its often strident tone—as a call for the school system to inculcate in black students, immigrants, and other minorities resentment and bitterness toward the chief institutions in American life.

The appearance of the Sobol report signals that an ideological struggle currently in progress in many elite universities is about to reach a new battlefield. Until now the struggle has been waged by left-of-center academics who challenge the idea that all students should be exposed to the classics of Western literature and philosophy. In such places as Stanford University, works like *The Wretched of the Earth* by Frantz Fanon, a paean to revolutionary violence, occupy a position in the core curriculum once reserved for the writings of Rousseau and John Stuart Mill. These issues are now to be contested in the domain of taxpayer-funded secondary education.

It is still early to gauge the prospects of the Sobol effort. When it appeared, there was little dissent to the report's tone or findings. Hamilton, its principal author, reports that all members of the Sobol task force signed off on it—that "everyone connected with the effort was very pleased." According to Hamilton, the initial response from New York's Board of Regents, the educational oversight body appointed by the state legislature, was also positive.

As things stand, the Sobol program *will* be implemented—unless major opposition emerges. Before the end of the year, Sobol is supposed to recommend action to the Regents, who will review the commissioner's recommendation in committee and, in January, will vote on whether and how to implement the report.

But changes of the sort that the Sobol report envisages cannot easily be implemented in public schools over the objection of parents and local politicians. It seems likely, for example, that Governor Mario Cuomo will want to distance himself from the Sobol report. Though the report's title is borrowed from one of Cuomo's favorite stump themes—"the politics of inclusion"—its content has little in common with the Governor's views.

It would be a mistake, by the way, to rea
right-left terms. Conservatives are hardly a
in the teaching of accurate, balanced histo
ciety suffers if an educational curriculum
advertently fosters interethnic strife. F
remember the reason the Sobol report
first place: the fact that many blacks
poorly in school. The report offers no
curricular changes would help in this
offer a theory.

THE REGENTS'

New York—The radicaliz
apace. A report recently issu
of Education Thomas S
Inclusion," opens with the
Asian Americans, Puerto
have all been the victim
pression that has charac
United States and the
No, this oppression do
to minorities, but in
"systematic bias tow
"a terribly damagin
can, Asian, Latino
calls for a totally
schools, in whic
concerns of pec
of all curricula
ostensibly om
matics mater
science an
culture."

[3]Repri
20-21. ©
10016. R

York
polic
er's
the R
for N
frame
invoke
icans, a
as invite
equal." S
report w
Chancello
that had ju
tion, decla
ceed with i

Unfortu
is any guide
plan on the l
than critical
contain some
minority expe
document, ste
The idea that
of self-esteem,
American," is n
call such figures
well as a host of
ucts of "Eurocen
ously. And why, i
esteem, have Jap
obviously been ad
groups to make pla
pression of *all* nor
overhaul.

Surprisingly, the
"multicultural" cont
types) in the presen
written from each mi
a serious attempt to b
of American society."

not solve the problem, because it is only "additive and not at the center of the endeavors." This is what the Task Force calls "Eurocentered multiculturalism." The mere inclusion of material on minority experience, no matter how extensive, "cannot counteract deeply rooted racist traditions in American culture. Merely adding marginal examples of 'other' cultures to an assumed dominant culture cannot reverse long established and entrenched policies and practices of that dominant culture. . . . The European American monocultural perspective prevails. Its value system and norms dominate."

Hence the report's inoffensive-sounding title, "A Curriculum of Inclusion," conceals a radical intent; it is not just greater inclusion of minority cultures the Task Force seeks, but the dismantling of the dominant culture. By the Orwellian magic of a name—"European American"—the national culture is transformed into an *ethnic* culture on the same level as all of America's minority cultures. Children will be taught that all cultures are to be "equally valued"; that the contributions of Puerto Ricans and Chinese and Iroquois are as important in the development of our society as America's historical mainstream culture. The truth or falseness of this idea is beside the point; we are dealing here with pure ideology—a call for permanent cultural revolution. "How can one value other cultures," asks one of the report's contributors, "if it is implicit that Anglo-conformity is what is valued and other cultures are tolerated and celebrated only when they do not interfere with the social order?"

Compared to this broad polemic, the actual problems the report identifies in current textbooks seem almost trivial. In fact, most of the omissions the report complains of (e.g., the Puerto Rican migration since World War II, the role of Chinese workers in building the transcontinental railroad, meaningful portraits of African Americans) seem to call for exactly the kind of expanded inclusiveness that its authors contemptuously dismiss as merely "additive." For the rest, the curricular review adds up to little more than a captious racial census of the *pictures* that appear in textbooks. Black Studies professor Leonard Jeffries writes: "Social Studies Program 3 does not include a *multicultural* illustration on the cover *as is done in volumes one and two* [emphasis added]; it depicts two European American youths in school activity." Jeffries criticizes another social-studies cover because, while it portrays white, Asian, and black families, the black family only includes a single parent. "A subtle message is thereby conveyed," writes Jeffries, "about differences in family structure in different cultures." One can't help thinking that if the cover had portrayed a black family with *two* parents, Jeffries would then have denounced it for imposing mainstream family models on inner-city blacks. One thing you can be sure of: the dominant culture is guilty no matter what it does.

This bias extends throughout the entire report. Among its suggestions for the social-studies curriculum, it recommends that the Age of Exploration be portrayed with a view to "negative values and policies that produced aggressive individuals and nations that were ready to 'discover, invade, and conquer' foreign land because of greed, racism, and national egoism." Meanwhile, the history of African Americans must be presented so that the heroic struggle for equity waged by African Americans can be an inspiration to all." Blacks during the American Revolution were fighting "strictly for freedom," while whites were only fighting to "protect their economic interest." So it goes.

The anti-white slant applies not just to what children shall be taught, but to the way children of different races shall be taught. In a discussion of the K-6 social-studies program—the current goals of which are to "decrease egocentric and stereotypical perceptions" and "increase the ability to empathize"—the Task Force remarks, with bureaucratic coyness: "Ironically, while these objectives apply broadly to all young people, African American, Asian American, Puerto Rican/Latino, and Native American children (because of ego starvation and negative socialization) have special needs that can be more meaningfully met by positive images and cultural experiences." Translation: We're going to tear down the egocentrism of whites (for their own good—to make them less "arrogant") while tendentiously increasing the self-esteem (read: ethnic chauvinism) of non-whites—a sort of affirmative action of the mind.

But not to worry. The report has added a reassuring caveat: "Aspects of cooperation and amicability among all cultures should be stressed over conflict and violence."

But one searches in vain for any sign of amicability in a document that is based on a race-oppression model of intellectual life. "The curriculum in the education systems reflects . . . deep-seated pathologies of racial hatred. . . . Because of the depth of the problem and the tenacity of its hold on the mind, *only the most stringent measures can have significant impact.*" Doesn't sound very amicable to me. But how could it be otherwise? Since "European American" culture is *by definition* exclusive and oppressive, it obviously cannot coexist with the oppressed cultures that seek equality with it until it has been stripped of its hypocritical pretensions to universality and legitimacy—i.e., until, as a national culture, it has ceased to exist.

The multiculturalist movement, in its totalist aims, is profoundly inimical to Western and liberal values. Yet, amazingly, it has managed to gain acceptance within the liberal establishment by retaining the aura of social justice, the patina of humanitarianism, that properly belongs to the older liberalism it has supplanted. How long are liberals and conservatives, both of whom oppose the traditional kinds of radicalism, going to keep on acquiescing in *cultural* radicalism?

A final note: On the train heading back to New York from the Regents' meeting in Albany, I struck up a conversation with a very bright young woman, a college senior majoring in English, who told me she was planning to be a teacher. She said she recently took an education course, "*but all we talked about each day was race. We didn't learn anything about education.*" She said the experience has made her think twice about her career aims. Now she thinks she might teach in private rather than public school—or perhaps not go into teaching at all.

MULTICULTURALISM[4]

Questions of race, ethnicity, and religion have been a perennial source of conflict in American education. The schools have often attracted the zealous attention of those who wish to influence the future, as well as those who wish to change the way we view the past. In our history, the schools have been not only an institution in which to teach young people skills and knowledge, but an arena where interest groups fight to preserve their values,

[4]Article by Diane Ravitch, author and adjunct professor of history and education at Columbia University's Teacher's College. Reprinted from *The American Scholar*, Number 3, Sum '90. 59: 337–54. Copyright © 1990 by Diane Ravitch. Reprinted with permission.

or to revise the judgments of history, or to bring about fundamental social change. In the nineteenth century, Protestants and Catholics battled over which version of the Bible should be used in school, or whether the Bible should be used at all. In recent decades, bitter racial disputes—provoked by policies of racial segregation and discrimination—have generated turmoil in the streets and in the schools. The secularization of the schools during the past century has prompted attacks on the curricula and textbooks and library books by fundamentalist Christians, who object to whatever challenges their faith-based views of history, literature, and science.

Given the diversity of American society, it has been impossible to insulate the schools from pressures that result from differences and tensions among groups. When people differ about basic values, sooner or later those disagreements turn up in battles about how schools are organized or what the schools should teach. Sometimes these battles remove a terrible injustice, like racial segregation. Sometimes, however, interest groups politicize the curriculum and attempt to impose their views on teachers, school officials, and textbook publishers. Across the country, even now, interest groups are pressuring local school boards to remove myths and fables and other imaginative literature from children's readers and to inject the teaching of creationism in biology. When groups cross the line into extremism, advancing their own agenda without regard to reason or to others, they threaten public education itself, making it difficult to teach any issues honestly and making the entire curriculum vulnerable to political campaigns.

For many years, the public schools attempted to neutralize controversies over race, religion, and ethnicity by ignoring them. Educators believed, or hoped, that the schools could remain outside politics; this was, of course, a vain hope since the schools were pursuing policies based on race, religion, and ethnicity. Nonetheless, such divisive questions were usually excluded from the curriculum. The textbooks minimized problems among groups and taught a sanitized version of history. Race, religion, and ethnicity were presented as minor elements in the American saga; slavery was treated as an episode, immigration as a sidebar, and women were largely absent. The textbooks concentrated on presidents, wars, national politics, and issues of state. An occasional "great black" or "great woman" received mention, but the main narrative paid little attention to minority groups and women.

With the ethnic revival of the 1960s, this approach to the teaching of history came under fire, because the history of national leaders—virtually all of whom were white, Anglo-Saxon, and male—ignored the place in American history of those who were none of the above. The traditional history of elites had been complemented by an assimilationist view of American society, which presumed that everyone in the American melting pot would eventually lose or abandon those ethnic characteristics that distinguished them from mainstream Americans. The ethnic revival demonstrated that many groups did not want to be assimilated or melted. Ethnic studies programs popped up on campuses to teach not only that "black is beautiful," but also that every other variety of ethnicity is "beautiful" as well; everyone who had "roots" began to look for them so that they too could recover that ancestral part of themselves that had not been homogenized.

As ethnicity became an accepted subject for study in the late 1960s, textbooks were assailed for their failure to portray blacks accurately; within a few years, the textbooks in wide use were carefully screened to eliminate bias against minority groups and women. At the same time, new scholarship about the history of women, blacks, and various ethnic minorities found its way into the textbooks. At first, the multicultural content was awkwardly incorporated as little boxes on the side of the main narrative. Then some of the new social historians (like Stephan Thernstrom, Mary Beth Norton, Gary Nash, Winthrop Jordan, and Leon Litwack) themselves wrote textbooks, and the main narrative itself began to reflect a broadened historical understanding of race, ethnicity, and class in the American past. Consequently, today's history textbooks routinely incorporate the experiences of women, blacks, American Indians, and various immigrant groups.

Although most high school textbooks are deeply unsatisfactory (they still largely neglect religion, they are too long, too encyclopedic, too superficial, and lacking in narrative flow), they are far more sensitive to pluralism than their predecessors. For example, the latest edition of Todd and Curti's *Triumph of the American Nation*, the most popular high school history text, has significantly increased its coverage of blacks in America, including profiles of Phillis Wheatley, the poet; James Armistead, a revolutionary war spy for Lafayette; Benjamin Banneker, a self-taught scientist and mathematician; Hiram Revels, the first black to serve in the

Congress; and Ida B. Wells-Barnett, a tireless crusader against lynching and racism. Even better as a textbook treatment is Jordan and Litwack's *The United States*, which skillfully synthesizes the historical experiences of blacks, Indians, immigrants, women, and other groups into the mainstream of American social and political history. The latest generation of textbooks bluntly acknowledges the racism of the past, describing the struggle for equality by racial minorities while identifying individuals who achieved success as political leaders, doctors, lawyers, scholars, entrepreneurs, teachers, and scientists.

As a result of the political and social changes of recent decades, cultural pluralism is now generally recognized as an organizing principle of this society. In contrast to the idea of the melting pot, which promised to erase ethnic and group differences, children now learn that variety is the spice of life. They learn that America has provided a haven for many different groups and has allowed them to maintain their cultural heritage or to assimilate, or—as is often the case—to do both; the choice is theirs, not the state's. They learn that cultural pluralism is one of the norms of a free society; that differences among groups are a national resource rather than a problem to be solved. Indeed, the unique feature of the United States is that its common culture has been formed by the interaction of its subsidiary cultures. It is a culture that has been influenced over time by immigrants, American Indians, Africans (slave and free) and by their descendants. American music, art, literature, language, food, clothing, sports, holidays, and customs all show the effects of the commingling of diverse cultures in one nation. Paradoxical though it may seem, the United States has a common culture that is multicultural.

Our schools and our institutions of higher learning have in recent years begun to embrace what Catherine R. Stimpson of Rutgers University has called "cultural democracy," a recognition that we must listen to a "diversity of voices" in order to understand our culture, past and present. This understanding of the pluralistic nature of American culture has taken a long time to forge. It is based on sound scholarship and has led to major revisions in what children are taught and what they read in school. The new history is—indeed, must be—a warts-and-all history; it demands an unflinching examination of racism and discrimination in our history. Making these changes is difficult, raises tempers, and ignites controversies, but gives a more interesting and accurate account of American history. Accomplishing these changes is valuable, because there is also a useful lesson for the rest of the world in America's relatively successful experience as a pluralistic society. Throughout human history, the clash of different cultures, races, ethnic groups, and religions has often been the cause of bitter hatred, civil conflict, and international war. The ethnic tensions that now are tearing apart Lebanon, Sri Lanka, Kashmir, and various republics of the Soviet Union remind us of the costs of unfettered group rivalry. Thus, it is a matter of more than domestic importance that we closely examine and try to understand that part of our national history in which different groups competed, fought, suffered, but ultimately learned to live together in relative peace and even achieved a sense of common nationhood.

Alas, these painstaking efforts to expand the understanding of American culture into a richer and more varied tapestry have taken a new turn, and not for the better. Almost any idea, carried to its extreme, can be made pernicious, and this is what is happening now to multiculturalism. Today, pluralistic multiculturalism must contend with a new, particularistic multiculturalism. The pluralists seek a richer common culture; the particularists insist that no common culture is possible or desirable. The new particularism is entering the curriculum in a number of school systems across the country. Advocates of particularism propose an ethnocentric curriculum to raise the self-esteem and academic achievement of children from racial and ethnic minority backgrounds. Without any evidence, they claim that children from minority backgrounds will do well in school *only* if they are immersed in a positive, prideful version of their ancestral culture. If children are of, for example, Fredonian ancestry, they must hear that Fredonians were important in mathematics, science, history, and literature. If they learn about great Fredonians and if their studies use Fredonian examples and Fredonian concepts, they will do well in school. If they do not, they will have low self-esteem and will do badly.

At first glance, this appears akin to the celebratory activities associated with Black History Month or Women's History Month, when schoolchildren learn about the achievements of blacks and women. But the point of those celebrations is to demonstrate that neither race nor gender is an obstacle to high achievement. They teach all children that everyone, regardless of their race, religion, gender, ethnicity, or family origin, can achieve self-fulfillment, honor, and dignity in society if they aim high and work hard.

By contrast, the particularistic version of multiculturalism is unabashedly filiopietistic and deterministic. It teaches children that their identity is determined by their "cultural genes." That something in their blood or their race memory or their cultural DNA defines who they are and what they may achieve. That the culture in which they live is not their own culture, even though they were born here. That American culture is "Eurocentric," and therefore hostile to anyone whose ancestors are not European. Perhaps the most invidious implication of particularism is that racial and ethnic minorities are not and should not try to be part of American culture; it implies that American culture belongs only to those who are white and European; it implies that those who are neither white nor European are alienated from American culture by virtue of their race or ethnicity; it implies that the only culture they do belong to or can ever belong to is the culture of their ancestors, even if their families have lived in this country for generations.

The war on so-called Eurocentrism is intended to foster self-esteem among those who are not of European descent. But how, in fact, is self-esteem developed? How is the sense of one's own possibilities, one's potential choices, developed? Certainly, the school curriculum plays a relatively small role as compared to the influence of family, community, mass media, and society. But to the extent that curriculum influences what children think of themselves, it should encourage children of all racial and ethnic groups to believe that they are part of this society and that they should develop their talents and minds to the fullest. It is enormously inspiring, for example, to learn about men and women from diverse backgrounds who overcame poverty, discrimination, physical handicaps, and other obstacles to achieve success in a variety of fields. Behind every such biography of accomplishment is a story of heroism, perseverance, and self-discipline. Learning these stories will encourage a healthy spirit of pluralism, of mutual respect, and of self-respect among children of different backgrounds. The children of American society today will live their lives in a racially and culturally diverse nation, and their education should prepare them to do so.

The pluralist approach to multiculturalism promotes a broader interpretation of the common American culture and seeks due recognition for the ways that the nation's many racial, ethnic, and cultural groups have transformed the national culture. The pluralists say, in effect, "American culture belongs to us, all of us; the U.S. is us, and we remake it in every generation." But particularists have no interest in extending or revising American culture; indeed, they deny that a common culture exists. Particularists reject any accommodation among groups, any interactions that blur the distinct lines between them. The brand of history that they espouse is one in which everyone is either a descendant of victims or oppressors. By doing so, ancient hatreds are fanned and recreated in each new generation. Particularism has its intellectual roots in the ideology of ethnic separatism and in the black nationalist movement. In the particularist analysis, the nation has five cultures: African American, Asian American, European American, Latino/Hispanic, and Native American. The huge cultural, historical, religious, and linguistic differences within these categories are ignored, as is the considerable intermarriage among these groups, as are the linkages (like gender, class, sexual orientation, and religion) that cut across these five groups. No serious scholar would claim that all Europeans and white Americans are part of the same culture, or that all Asians are part of the same culture, or that all people of Latin-American descent are of the same culture, or that all people of African descent are of the same culture. Any categorization this broad is essentially meaningless and useless.

Several districts—including Detroit, Atlanta, and Washington, D.C.—are developing an Afrocentric curriculum. *Afrocentricity* has been described in a book of the same name by Molefi Kete Asante of Temple University. The Afrocentric curriculum puts Africa at the center of the student's universe. African Americans must "move away from an [*sic*] Eurocentric framework" because "it is difficult to create freely when you use someone else's motifs, styles, images, and perspectives." Because they are not Africans, "white teachers cannot inspire in our children the visions necessary for them to overcome limitations." Asante recommends that African Americans choose an African name (as he did), reject European dress, embrace African religion (not Islam or Christianity) and love "their own" culture. He scorns the idea of universality as a form of Eurocentric arrogance.

The Eurocentrist, he says, thinks of Beethoven or Bach as classical, but the Afrocentrist thinks of Ellington or Coltrane as classical; the Eurocentrist lauds Shakespeare or Twain, while the Afrocentrist prefers Baraka, Shange, or Abiola. Asante is critical of black artists like Arthur Mitchell and Alvin Ailey who ignore Afrocentricity. Likewise, he speaks contemptuously of a group of black university students who spurned the Afrocentrism of the local Black Student Union and formed an organization called Interrace: "Such madness is the direct consequence of self-hatred, obligatory attitudes, false assumptions about society, and stupidity."

The conflict between pluralism and particularism turns on the issue of universalism. Professor Asante warns his readers against the lure of universalism: "Do not be captured by a sense of universality given to you by the Eurocentric viewpoint; such a viewpoint is contradictory to your own ultimate reality." He insists that there is no alternative to Eurocentrism, Afrocentrism, and other ethnocentrisms. In contrast, the pluralist says, with the Roman playwright Terence, "I am a man: nothing human is alien to me." A contemporary Terence would say "I am a person" or might be a woman, but the point remains the same: You don't have to be black to love Zora Neale Hurston's fiction or Langston Hughes's poetry or Duke Ellington's music. In a pluralist curriculum, we expect children to learn a broad and humane culture, to learn about the ideas and art and animating spirit of many cultures. We expect that children, whatever their color, will be inspired by the courage of people like Helen Keller, Vaclav Havel, Harriet Tubman, and Feng Lizhe. We expect that their response to literature will be determined by the ideas and images it evokes, not by the skin color of the writer. But particularists insist that children can learn only from the experiences of people from the same race.

Particularism is a bad idea whose time has come. It is also a fashion spreading like wildfire through the education system, actively promoted by organizations and individuals with a political and professional interest in strengthening ethnic power bases in the university, in the education profession, and in society itself. One can scarcely pick up an educational journal without learning about a school district that is converting to an ethnocentric curriculum in an attempt to give "self-esteem" to children from racial minorities. A state-funded project in a Sacramento high school is teaching young black males to think like Africans and to develop the "African Mind Model Technique," in order to free themselves of the racism of American culture. A popular black rap singer, KRS-One, complained in an op-ed article in the *New York Times* that the schools should be teaching blacks about their cultural heritage, instead of trying to make everyone Americans. "It's like trying to teach a dog to be a cat," he wrote. KRS-One railed about having to learn about Thomas Jefferson and the Civil War, which had nothing to do (he said) with black history.

Pluralism can easily be transformed into particularism, as may be seen in the potential uses in the classroom of the Mayan contribution to mathematics. The Mayan example was popularized in a movie called *Stand and Deliver*, about a charismatic Bolivian-born mathematics teacher in Los Angeles who inspired his students (who are Hispanic) to learn calculus. He told them that their ancestors invented the concept of zero; but that wasn't all he did. He used imagination to put across mathematical concepts. He required them to do homework and to go to school on Saturdays and during the Christmas holidays, so that they might pass the Advanced Placement mathematics examination for college entry. The teacher's reference to the Mayans' mathematical genius was a valid instructional device: It was an attention-getter and would have interested even students who were not Hispanic. But the Mayan example would have had little effect without the teacher's insistence that the class study hard for a difficult examination.

Ethnic educators have seized upon the Mayan contribution to mathematics as the key to simultaneously boosting the ethnic pride of Hispanic children and attacking Eurocentrism. One proposal claims that Mexican-American children will be attracted to science and mathematics if they study Mayan mathematics, the Mayan calendar, and Mayan astronomy. Children in primary grades are to be taught that the Mayans were first to discover the zero and that Europeans learned it long afterwards from the Arabs, who had learned it in India. This will help them see that Europeans were latecomers in the discovery of great ideas. Botany is to be learned by study of the agricultural techniques of the Aztecs, a subject of somewhat limited relevance to children in urban areas. Furthermore, "ethnobotanical" classifications of plants are to be substituted for the Eurocentric Linnaean system. At first glance, it may seem curious that Hispanic children are deemed to have no cultural affinity with Spain; but to acknowledge the cultural tie would confuse the ideological assault on Eurocentrism.

This proposal suggests some questions: Is there any evidence that the teaching of "culturally relevant" science and mathematics will draw Mexican-American children to the study of these subjects? Will Mexican-American children lose interest or self-esteem if they discover that their ancestors were Aztecs or Spaniards, rather than Mayans? Are children who learn in this way prepared to study the science and mathematics that are taught in American colleges and universities and that are needed for advanced study in these fields? Are they even prepared to study the science and mathematics taught in *Mexican* universities? If the class is half Mexican-American and half something else, will only the Mexican-American children study in a Mayan and Aztec mode or will all the children? But shouldn't all children study what is culturally relevant for them? How will we train teachers who have command of so many different systems of mathematics and science?

The efficacy of particularist proposals seems to be less important to their sponsors than their value as ideological weapons with which to criticize existing disciplines for their alleged Eurocentric bias. In a recent article titled "The Ethnocentric Basis of Social Science Knowledge Production" in the *Review of Research in Education*, John Stanfield of Yale University argues that neither social science nor science are objective studies, that both instead are "Euro-American" knowledge systems which reproduce "hegemonic racial domination." The claim that science and reason are somehow superior to magic and witchcraft, he writes, is the product of Euro-American ethnocentrism. According to Stanfield, current fears about the misuse of science (for instance, "the nuclear arms race, global pollution") and "the power-plays of Third World nations (the Arab oil boycott and the American-Iranian hostage crisis) have made Western people more aware of nonscientific cognitive styles. These last events are beginning to demonstrate politically that which has begun to be understood in intellectual circles: namely, that modes of social knowledge such as theology, science, and magic are different, not inferior or superior. They represent different ways of perceiving, defining, and organizing knowledge of life experiences." One wonders: If Professor Stanfield broke his leg, would he go to a theologian, a doctor, or a magician?

Every field of study, it seems, has been tainted by Eurocentrism, which was defined by a professor at Manchester University, George Ghevarughese Joseph, in *Race and Class* in 1987, as "intellectual racism." Professor Joseph argues that the history of science and technology—and in particular, of mathematics—in non-European societies was distorted by racist Europeans who wanted to establish the dominance of European forms of knowledge. The racists, he writes, traditionally traced mathematics to the Greeks, then claimed that it reached its full development in Europe. These are simply Eurocentric myths to sustain an "imperialist/racist ideology," says Professor Joseph, since mathematics was found in Egypt, Babylonia, Mesopotamia, and India long before the Greeks were supposed to have developed it. Professor Joseph points out too that Arab scientists should be credited with major discoveries traditionally attributed to William Harvey, Isaac Newton, Charles Darwin, and Sir Francis Bacon. But he is not concerned only to argue historical issues; his purpose is to bring all of these different mathematical traditions into the school classroom so that children might study, for example, "traditional African designs, Indian *rangoli* patterns and Islamic art" and "the language and counting systems found across the world."

This interesting proposal to teach ethnomathematics comes at a time when American mathematics educators are trying to overhaul present practices, because of the poor performance of American children on national and international assessments. Mathematics educators are attempting to change the teaching of their subject so that children can see its uses in everyday life. There would seem to be an incipient conflict between those who want to introduce real-life applications of mathematics and those who want to teach the mathematical systems used by ancient cultures. I suspect that most mathematics teachers would enjoy doing a bit of both, if there were time or student interest. But any widespread movement to replace modern mathematics with ancient ethnic mathematics runs the risk of disaster in a field that is struggling to update existing curricula. If, as seems likely, ancient mathematics is taught mainly to minority children, the gap between them and middle-class white children is apt to grow. It is worth noting that children in Korea, who score highest in mathematics on international assessments, do not study ancient Korean mathematics.

Particularism is akin to cultural Lysenkoism, for it takes as its premise the spurious notion that cultural traits are inherited. It implies a dubious, dangerous form of cultural predestination. Children are taught that if their ancestors could do it, so could they. But what happens if a child is from a cultural group that made no significant contribution to science or mathematics? Does this mean that children from that background must find a culturally appropriate field in which to strive? How does a teacher find the right cultural buttons for children of mixed heritage? And how in the world will teachers use this technique when the children in their classes are drawn from many different cultures, as is usually the case? By the time that every culture gets its due, there may be no time left to teach the subject itself. This explosion of filiopietism (which, we should remember, comes from adults, not from students) is reminiscent of the period some years ago when the Russians claimed that they had invented everything first; as we now know, this nationalistic braggadocio did little for their self-esteem and nothing for their economic development. We might reflect, too, on how little social prestige has been accorded in this country to immigrants from Greece and Italy, even though the achievements of their ancestors were at the heart of the classical curriculum.

Filiopietism and ethnic boosterism lead to all sorts of odd practices. In New York State, for example, the curriculum guide for eleventh grade American history lists three "foundations" for the United States Constitution, as follows:

A. Foundations
   1. 17th and 18th century Enlightenment thought
   2. Haudenosaunee political system
      a. Influence upon colonial leadership and European intellectuals (Locke, Montesquieu, Voltaire, Rousseau)
      b. Impact on Albany Plan of Union, Articles of Confederation, and U.S. Constitution
   3. Colonial experience

Those who are unfamiliar with the Haudenosaunee political system might wonder what it is, particularly since educational authorities in New York State rank it as equal in importance to the European Enlightenment and suggest that it strongly influenced not only colonial leaders but the leading intellectuals of Europe. The Haudenosaunee political system was the Iroquois confederation of five (later six) Indian tribes in upper New York State, which conducted war and civil affairs through a council of chiefs, each with one vote. In 1754, Benjamin Franklin proposed a colonial union at a conference in Albany; his plan, said to be inspired by the Iroquois Confederation, was rejected by the other colonies. Today, Indian activists believe that the Iroquois Confederation was the model for the American Constitution, and the New York State Department of Education has decided that they are right. That no other state sees fit to give the American Indians equal billing with the European Enlightenment may be owing to the fact that the Indians in New York State (numbering less than forty thousand) have been more politically effective than elsewhere or that other states have not yet learned about this method of reducing "Eurocentrism" in their American history classes.

Particularism can easily be carried to extremes. Students of Fredonian descent must hear that their ancestors were seminal in the development of all human civilization and that without the Fredonian contribution, we would all be living in caves or trees, bereft of art, technology, and culture. To explain why Fredonians today are in modest circumstances, given their historic eminence, children are taught that somewhere, long ago, another culture stole the Fredonians' achievements, palmed them off as their own, and then oppressed the Fredonians.

I first encountered this argument almost twenty years ago, when I was a graduate student. I shared a small office with a young professor, and I listened as she patiently explained to a student why she had given him a D on a term paper. In his paper, he argued that the Arabs had stolen mathematics from the Nubians in the desert long ago (I forget in which century this theft allegedly occurred). She tried to explain to him about the necessity of historical evidence. He was unconvinced, since he believed that he had uncovered a great truth that was beyond proof. The part I couldn't understand was how anyone could lose knowledge by sharing it. After all, cultures are constantly influencing one another, exchanging ideas and art and technology, and the exchange usually is enriching, not depleting.

Today, there are a number of books and articles advancing controversial theories about the origins of civilization. An important work, *The African Origin of Civilization: Myth or Reality*, by Senegalese scholar Cheikh Anta Diop, argues that ancient Egypt was a black civilization, that all races are descended from the black race, and that the achievements of "western" civilization originated in Egypt. The views of Diop and other Africanists have been condensed into an everyman's paperback titled *What They Never Told You in History Class* by Indus Khamit Kush. This latter book claims that Moses, Jesus, Buddha, Mohammed, and Vishnu were Africans; that the first Indians, Chinese, Hebrews, Greeks, Romans, Britains, and Americans were Africans; and that the first mathematicians, scientists, astronomers, and physicians were Africans. A debate currently raging among some classicists is whether the Greeks "stole" the philosophy, art, and religion of the ancient Egyptians and whether the ancient Egyptians were black Africans. George G. M. James's *Stolen Legacy* insists that the Greeks "stole the Legacy of the African Continent and called it their own." James argues that the civilization of Greece, the vaunted foundation of European culture, owed everything it knew and did to its African predecessors. Thus, the roots of western civilization lies not in Greece and Rome, but in Egypt and, ultimately, in black Africa.

Similar speculation was fueled by the publication in 1987 of Martin Bernal's *Black Athena: The Afroasiatic Roots of Classical Civilization*, Volume 1, *The Fabrication of Ancient Greece, 1785–1985*, although the controversy predates Bernal's book. In a fascinating foray into the politics of knowledge, Bernal attributes the preference of Western European scholars for Greece over Egypt as the fount of knowledge to nearly two centuries of racism and "Europocentrism," but he is uncertain about the color of the ancient Egyptians. However, a review of Bernal's book last year in the *Village Voice* began, "What color were the ancient Egyptians? Blacker than Mubarak, baby." The same article claimed that white racist archeologists chiseled the noses off ancient Egyptian statues so that future generations would not see the typically African facial characteristics. The debate reached the pages of the *Biblical Archeology Review* last year in an article titled "Were the Ancient Egyptians Black or White?" The author, classicist Frank J. Yurco, argues that some Egyptian rulers were black, others were not, and that "the ancient Egyptians did not think in these terms." The issue, wrote Yurco, "is a chimera, cultural baggage from our own society that can only be imposed artificially on ancient Egyptian society."

Most educationists are not even aware of the debate about whether the ancient Egyptians were black or white, but they are very sensitive to charges that the schools' curricula are Eurocentric, and they are eager to rid the schools of the taint of Eurocentrism. It is hardly surprising that America's schools would recognize strong cultural ties with Europe since our nation's political, religious, educational, and economic institutions were created chiefly by people of European descent, our government was shaped by European ideas, and nearly 80 percent of the people who live here are of European descent. The particularists treat all of this history as a racist bias toward Europe, rather than as the matter-of-fact consequences of European immigration. Even so, American education is not centered on Europe. American education, if it is centered on anything, is centered on itself. It is "Americentric." Most American students today have never studied any world history; they know very little about Europe, and even less about the rest of the world. Their minds are rooted solidly in the here and now. When the Berlin Wall was opened in the fall of 1989, journalists discovered that most American teenagers had no idea what it was, nor why its opening was such a big deal. Nonetheless, Eurocentrism provides a better target than Americentrism.

In school districts where most children are black and Hispanic, there has been a growing tendency to embrace particularism rather than pluralism. Many of the children in these districts perform poorly in academic classes and leave school without graduating. They would fare better in school if they had well-educated and well-paid teachers, small classes, good materials, encouragement at home and school, summer academic programs, protection from the drugs and crime that ravage their neighborhoods, and higher expectations of satisfying careers upon graduation. These are expensive and time-consuming remedies that must also engage the large society beyond the school. The lure of particularism is that it offers a less complicated anodyne, one in which the children's academic deficiencies may be addressed—or set aside—by inflating their racial pride. The danger of this remedy is that it will detract attention from the real needs of schools and the real interests of children, while simultaneously arousing distorted race pride in children of all races, increasing racial antagonism and producing fresh recruits for white and black racist groups.

The particularist critique gained a major forum in New York in 1989, with the release of a report called "A Curriculum of Inclusion," produced by a task force created by the State Commissioner of Education, Thomas Sobol. In 1987, soon after his appointment, Sobol appointed a Task Force on Minorities to review the state's curriculum for instances of bias. He did this not because there had been complaints about bias in the curriculum, but because—as a newly appointed state commissioner whose previous job had been to superintend the public schools of a wealthy suburb, Scarsdale—he wanted to demonstrate his sensitivity to minority concerns. The Sobol task force was composed of representatives of African American, Hispanic, Asian American, and American Indian groups.

The task force engaged four consultants, one from each of the aforementioned racial or ethnic minorities, to review nearly one hundred teachers' guides prepared by the state. These guides define the state's curriculum, usually as a list of facts and concepts to be taught, along with model activities. The primary focus of the consultants, not surprisingly, was the history and social studies curriculum. As it happened, the history curriculum had been extensively revised in 1987 to make it multicultural, in both American and world history. In the 1987 revision the time given to Western Europe was reduced to one-quarter of one year, as part of a two-year global studies sequence in which equal time was allotted to seven major world regions, including Africa and Latin America.

As a result of the 1987 revisions in American and world history, New York State had one of the most advanced multicultural history-social studies curricula in the country. Dozens of social studies teachers and consultants had participated, and the final draft was reviewed by such historians as Eric Foner of Columbia University, the late Hazel Hertzberg of Teachers College, Columbia University, and Christopher Lasch of the University of Rochester. The curriculum was overloaded with facts, almost to the point of numbing students with details and trivia, but it was not insensitive to ethnicity in American history or unduly devoted to European history.

But the Sobol task force decided that this curriculum was biased and Eurocentric. The first sentence of the task force report summarizes its major thesis: "African Americans, Asian Americans, Puerto Ricans/Latinos, and Native Americans have all been the victims of an intellectual and educational oppression that has characterized the culture and institutions of the United States and the European American world for centuries."

The task force report was remarkable in that it vigorously denounced bias without identifying a single instance of bias in the curricular guides under review. Instead, the consultants employed harsh, sometimes inflammatory, rhetoric to treat every difference of opinion or interpretation as an example of racial bias. The African-American consultant, for example, excoriates the curriculum for its "White Anglo-Saxon (WASP) value system and norms," its "deep-seated pathologies of racial hatred" and its "white nationalism"; he decries as bias the fact that children study Egypt as part of the Middle East instead of as part of Africa. Perhaps Egypt should be studied as part of the African unit (geographically, it is located on the African continent); but placing it in one region rather than the other is not what most people think of as racism or bias. The "Latino" consultant criticizes the use of the term "Spanish-American War" instead of "Spanish-Cuban-American War." The Native American consultant complains that tribal languages are classified as "foreign languages."

The report is consistently Europhobic. It repeatedly expresses negative judgments on "European Americans" and on everything Western and European. All people with a white skin are referred to as "Anglo-Saxons" and "WASPs." Europe, says the report, is uniquely responsible for producing aggressive individuals who "were ready to 'discover, invade and conquer' foreign land because of greed, racism and national egoism." All white people are held collectively guilty for the historical crimes of slavery and racism. There is no mention of the "Anglo-Saxons" who opposed slavery and racism. Nor does the report acknowledge that some whites have been victims of discrimination and oppression. The African American consultant writes of the Constitution, "There is something vulgar and revolting in glorifying a process that heaped undeserved rewards on a segment of the population while oppressing the majority."

The New York task force proposal is not merely about the reconstruction of what is taught. It goes a step further to suggest that the history curriculum nay be used to ensure that "children from Native American, Puerto Rican/Latino, Asian American, and African American cultures will have higher self-esteem and self-respect, while children from European cultures will have a less arrogant perspective of being part of the group that has 'done it all.'"

In February 1990, Commissioner Sobol asked the New York Board of Regents to endorse a sweeping revision of the history curriculum to make it more multicultural. His recommendations were couched in measured tones, not in the angry rhetoric of his task force. The board supported his request unanimously. It remains to be seen whether New York pursues the particularist path marked out by the Commissioner's advisory group or finds its way to the concept of pluralism within a democratic tradition.

The rising tide of particularism encourages the politicization of all curricula in the schools. If education bureaucrats bend to the political and ideological winds, as is their wont, we can anticipate a generation of struggle over the content of the curriculum in mathematics, science, literature, and history. Demands for "culturally relevant" studies, for ethnostudies of all kinds, will open the classroom to unending battles over whose version is taught, who gets credit for what, and which ethno-interpretation is appropriate. Only recently have districts begun to resist the demands of fundamentalist groups to censor textbooks and library books (and some have not yet begun to do so).

The spread of particularism throws into question the very idea of American public education. Public schools exist to teach children the general skills and knowledge that they need to succeed in American society, and the specific skills and knowledge that they need in order to function as American citizens. They receive public support because they have a public function. Historically, the public schools were known as "common schools" because they were schools for all, even if the children of all the people did not attend them. Over the years, the courts have found that it was unconstitutional to teach religion in the common schools, or to separate children on the basis of their race in the common schools. In their curriculum, their hiring practices, and their general philosophy, the public schools must not discriminate against or give preference to any racial or ethnic group. Yet they are permitted to accommodate cultural diversity by, for example, serving food that is culturally appropriate or providing library collections that emphasize the interests of the local community. However, they should not be expected to teach children to view the world through an ethnocentric perspective that rejects or ignores the common culture. For generations, those groups that wanted to inculcate their religion or their ethnic heritage have instituted private schools—after school, on weekends, or on a full-time basis. There, children learn with others of the same group—Greeks, Poles, Germans, Japanese, Chinese, Jews, Lutherans, Catholics, and so on—and are taught by people from the same group. Valuable as this exclusive experience has been for those who chose it, this has not been the role of public education. One of the primary purposes of public education has been to create a national community, a definition of citizenship and culture that is both expansive and *inclusive*.

The curriculum in public schools must be based on whatever knowledge and practices have been determined to be best by professionals—experienced teachers and scholars—who are competent to make these judgments. Professional societies must be prepared to defend the integrity of their disciplines. When called upon, they should establish review committees to examine disputes over curriculum and to render judgment, in order to help school officials fend off improper political pressure. Where genuine controversies exist, they should be taught and debated in the classroom. Was Egypt a black civilization? Why not raise the question, read the arguments of the different sides in the debate, show slides of Egyptian pharoahs and queens, read books about life in ancient Egypt, invite guest scholars from the local university, and visit museums with Egyptian collections? If scholars disagree, students should know it. One great advantage of this approach is that students will see that history is a lively study, that textbooks are fallible, that historians disagree, that the writing of history is influenced by the historian's politics and ideology, that history is written by people who make choices among alternative facts and interpretations, and that history changes as new facts are uncovered and new interpretations win adherents. They will also learn that cultures and civilizations constantly interact, exchange ideas, and influence one another, and that the idea of racial or ethnic purity is a myth. Another advantage is that students might once again study ancient history, which has all but disappeared from the curricula of American schools. (California recently introduced a required sixth grade course in ancient civilizations, but ancient history is otherwise *terra incognita* in American education.)

The multicultural controversy may do wonders for the study of history, which has been neglected for years in American schools. At this time, only half of our high school graduates ever study any world history. Any serious attempt to broaden students' knowledge of Africa, Europe, Asia, and Latin America will require at least two, and possibly three years of world history (a requirement thus far only in California). American history, too, will need more time that the one-year high-school survey course. Those of us who have insisted for years on the importance of history in the curriculum may not be ready to assent to its redemptive power, but hope that our new allies will ultimately join a constructive dialogue that strengthens the place of history in the schools.

As cultural controversies arise, educators must adhere to the principle of "E Pluribus Unum." That is, they must maintain a balance between the demands of the one—the nation of which we are common citizens—and the many—the varied histories of the American people. It is not necessary to denigrate either the one or the many. Pluralism is a positive value, but it is also important that we preserve a sense of an American community—a society and a culture to which we all belong. If there is no overall community with an agreed-upon vision of liberty and justice; if all we have is a collection of racial and ethnic cultures, lacking any common bonds, then we have no means to mobilize public opinion on behalf of people who are not members of our particular group. We have, for example, no reason to support public education. If there is no larger community, then each group will want to teach its own children in its own way, and public education ceases to exist.

History should not be confused with filiopietism. History gives no grounds for race pride. No race has a monopoly on virtue. If anything, a study of history should inspire humility, rather than pride. People of every racial group have committed terrible crimes, often against others of the same group. Whether one looks at the history of Europe or Africa or Latin America or Asia, every continent offers examples of inhumanity. Slavery has existed in civilizations around the world for centuries. Examples of genocide can be found around the world, throughout history, from ancient times right through to our own day. Governments and cultures, sometimes by edict, sometimes simply following tradition, have practiced not only slavery, but human sacrifice, infanticide, cliterodectomy, and mass murder. If we teach children this, they might recognize how absurd both racial hatred and racial chauvinism are.

What must be preserved in the study of history is the spirit of inquiry, the readiness to open new questions and to pursue new understandings. History, at its best, is a search for truth. The best way to portray this search is through debate and controversy, rather than through imposition of fixed beliefs and immutable facts. Perhaps the most dangerous aspect of school history is its tendency to become Official History, a sanctified version of the Truth taught by the state to captive audiences and embedded in beautiful mass-market textbooks as holy writ. When Official History is written by committees responding to political pressures, rather than by scholars synthesizing the best available research, then the errors of the past are replaced by the politically fashionable errors of the present. It may be difficult to teach children that history is both important and uncertain, and that even the best historians never have all the pieces of the jigsaw puzzle, but it is necessary to do so. If state education departments permit the revision of their history courses and textbooks to become an exercise in power politics, then the entire process of state-level curriculum-making becomes suspect, as does public education itself.

The question of self-esteem is extraordinarily complex, and it goes well beyond the content of the curriculum. Most of what we call self-esteem is formed in the home and in a variety of life experiences, not only in school. Nonetheless, it has been important for blacks—and for other racial groups—to learn about the history of slavery and of the civil rights movement; it has been important for blacks to know that their ancestors actively resisted enslavement and actively pursued equality; and it has been important for blacks and others to learn about black men and women who fought courageously against racism and who provide models of courage, persistence, and intellect. These are instances where the content of the curriculum reflects sound scholarship, and at the same time probably lessens racial prejudice and provides inspiration for those who are descendants of slaves. But knowing about the travails and triumphs of one's forebears does not necessarily translate into either self-esteem or personal accomplishment. For most children, self-esteem—the self-confidence that grows out of having reached a goal—comes not from hearing about the monuments of their ancestors but as a consequence of what they are able to do and accomplish through their own efforts.

As I reflected on these issues, I recalled reading an interview a few years ago with a talented black runner. She said that her model is Mikhail Baryshnikov. She admires him because he is a magnificent athlete. He is not black; he is not female; he is not American-born; he is not even a runner. But he inspires her because of the way he trained and used his body. When I read this, I thought how narrow-minded it is to believe that people can be inspired *only* by those who are exactly like them in race and ethnicity.

STRATEGIES FOR A DIVERSE AND COMPETITIVE AMERICA[5]

Thank you very much. It is a an honor to be here today for this important and timely conference. In the next half hour, I intend to touch on two primary subjects: first, a brief summary of the Business-Higher Education Forum's recent report on minority life in America; and second, an update on our more recent work, which has identified some major gaps between what the *experts* are thinking about such issues as education reform and adult literacy—and what the *public* is thinking about these subjects. As we shall explore, these gaps might have grave implications for *all of us* involved in workforce issues.

But first, a bit of background. It is a great pleasure to return to my home state of California. I left Sacremento almost twenty years ago to settle in Washington, D.C.

So, I feel a lot more comfortable taking a *national* perspective on the topic of today's conference. I am sure there is nothing I could tell you about California that you do not already know. Indeed, I have learned a lot already from this morning's sessions, and look forward to continuing my education this afternoon after lunch.

[5]Reprint of an speech by Don M. Blandin, Director, Business-Higher Education Forum, American Counsel on Education, delivered at the Conference on Workforce Diversity and Economic Competitiveness in Sacramento, October 1990. Vital Speeches of the Day © 1990 City News Publishing Co. Reprinted with permission of author.

Let me begin with a few statistics, to help set the stage for the rest of my remarks. In the past few decades—and especially in the past ten years—a nation comprised primarily of people of European descent has taken in millions and millions of Hispanics and Asians. In 1987 *alone*, nearly 150,000 Latin Americans, more than one hundred thousand people from the Caribbean islands, and over a quarter of a million Asians came to the U.S. to stay.

No state has felt the impact of immigration more than California. The new diversity of California—and of the nation—has reverberated through every social institution, including schools, state assemblies, and churches—changing the way we think about ourselves as Americans and challenging long-held notions of who we are.

But the changing ethnic makeup of America has been felt nowhere more keenly than in our offices and factories. In fact, over the past few decades, the American workplace has become *even more* ethnically and racially diverse than the nation as a whole, because African-American citizens have gained access to jobs and opportunities that were denied them for decades.

Today, 42 percent of new labor force entrants are either immigrants or minorities. That mega-trend, which is reshaping both the color and the cultural background of our workforce, presents real challenges on a daily basis to those of you who must manage these workers.

For example, one of Digital Equipment Company's factories in Boston employs 350 people from 44 countries, and they speak 19 languages. Written announcements are printed in Chinese, French, Spanish, Portuguese, Vietnamese and Haitian Creole, not to mention English. In the new lexicon, America's workplaces are fast becoming "multicultural" and "multiracial."

However, diversity on the factory floor has yet to catch up to the corner office. According to the Equal Employment Opportunity Commission, only 27 percent of all business managers are women, and a meager 9.5 percent are minorities. Only one CEO from *Business Week's* "Corporate Elite" is black. One is Hispanic, and only one is from the real majority-that is to say, only one is from the *real* majority—that is to say, only one is a woman. Three are Asian-Americans. That's out of *1000* corporate CEOs. That means about 99 percent of the occupants of the executive suites of America's largest companies are white males.

Adjusting to the new diversity in American society and the nations's workplaces is problematic. Not only are there unavoidable linguistic differences and cultural disparities between different ethnic and racial groups , even talking about race or cultural background in America can be tricky.

For example, consider two simple "facts"—quote, end quote—about race and ethnicity in America. First, Hispanics are far more likely to drop out of high school than whites. And second, a black male child born in California in 1988 is three times as likely to be murdered as he is to be admitted to the University of California.

Those and other probabilities and averages, although often true, give the impression that some minorities are indifferent to education, while others are uniformly caught up in crime.

And they mask a more important reality: within minority groups there is extraordinary diversity.

Just as understanding the average daily temperature in the continental United States does not prepare the visitor for August heat or January frost, so, too, understanding the average situation for members of minority groups does not illuminate the diversity of minority life in this country.

To improve America's understanding about diversity within minority groups, the Business-Higher Education Forum earlier this year completed a long and intensive study. Our report—entitled *Three Realities*: *Minority Life in the United States*—cuts through the stereotypical thinking that dominates so many assessments of American minorities. The report, which I believe all of you received, dissects the broad averages and reveals a more complex portrait of minority life.

I think it can help all of us understand the scope of the diversity we genuinely face in our workplaces.

The Forum undertook its analysis because we hoped to clarify the public debate about minority progress in the United States. As I mentioned, most discussions about minorities are based on the assumption that *all* minorities are poor, illiterate, or down-and-out—except for a handful of multi-million-dollar athletes and entertainers, like Michael Jordan and Bill Cosby.

Clearly, many minorities *are poor*. But when the minority experience is framed in such stark, universal terms, the problems almost always seem insurmountable. And the proposed solutions appear hopelessly inadequate.

In our view, by becoming preoccupied with problems and ignoring occasional progress, we have reinforced worst-case stereotypes and denied ourselves the necessity of hope. We have also
closed off analysis of the minorities who have made it, to see if
their experiences offer lessons for others.

The good news is that the Forum found a sound basis for
hope about the prospects for minorities in American life—that
it is wrongheaded to focus only on the negative.

The first of the three realities the Forum uncovered was that
a significant number of American minorities indeed are *making
it.* They are finishing high school, completing college, and entering careers that offer opportunities for economic advancement.

The good news is that the black middle class has expanded
rapidly during the past 30 years. In 1960, 13 percent of black
families earned middle-class incomes. By 1980, the proportion
reached 40 percent and climbed steadily throughout the decade.

Forty-four percent of black Americans own homes, and 1.5
million blacks work as managers, business executives and professionals. There are now more than 7000 black elected officials in
the United States, including more than 300 mayors.

Hispanic-Americans are not being universally left behind, either. Hispanics are much more likely to be recent immigrants to
the United States—in fact, the Census Bureau did not even begin
identifying Spanish-speaking peoples as a distinct American ethnic group until 1970. Nonetheless, 40 percent of Hispanics own
homes, and more than a third earn middle-class incomes.

Moreover, many Hispanics are repeating the pattern of earlier European immigrants: they arrive with little education or skills
and work hard so that their children can enjoy a better life. More
than half of all Mexican-born immigrants have less than a ninth-
grade education, but more than 40 percent of the *children* of these
immigrants attend college.

But the Forum's study found *three* realities for American minorities. The remaining *two* are not nearly so encouraging.

The second reality is that vast numbers of American minorities live right at the margin. These people possess few skills and
often hold jobs as laborers, farm workers, or domestics. About a
third of both blacks and Hispanics have incomes below $25,000
per year, but above $10,000, the offical poverty line. They live
paycheck to paycheck and can easily tumble into the ranks of the
impoverished.

The elimination of millions of low-skilled production jobs affects this group most directly, because those left without jobs after a plant closing are often too poorly skilled or educated to take a position in the emerging high-tech workplace. Xerox Chairman David Kearns, for example, likes to point out that at the end of World War II, a Navy cruiser required 1700 sailors, and the average education level needed to run the ship was eighth grade. Today a crusier has 700 sailors and the average education level is about two years beyond high school.

American business has undergone the same change, but for minorities at the margin that change has meant the elimination of jobs that provided them a reliable and reasonably decent income. Without sound cognitive skills, finding a new niche in the workplace has been difficult.

Critics might charge that what is true for blacks and Hispanics with few skills is true also for poorly skilled whites—that race is a shield used to cover the pain resulting from simple economic change. Obviously, millions of white Americans also live on the edge.

Admittedly, many blacks, Hispanics *and whites* may share a common economic fate, but minorities must also cope with racism. As a result, minorities at the margin are more likely to suffer longer periods of unemployment than whites of similar educational background and economic status.

The third reality about minority life in the United States is the most disturbing—that is the existence of *severe minority poverty*. This is perhaps the most enduring domestic challenge for our nation.

About one-third of all black families and one-quarter of all Hispanics earn less than $10,000 per year. Most live in cities where no imagination can stretch $10,000 into a living wage. And most are very poorly educated and thus very vulnerable to any change that affects their jobs—if they are employable at all.

But even within this poorest group of minorities there are important differences. It is important, for example, to understand the particular problems faced by a segment of the persistently poor termed the "underclass." Urban Institute analyst Isabel Sawhill undertook a careful study of the underclass and indentified 880 underclass neighborhoods in the United States.

The communities were overwhelmingly occupied by young people simultaneously battling poverty, illiteracy, family breakdown, unemployment, welfare dependency, crime, drug abuse, teen pregnancy and racial discrimination. Two-and-one-half million people lived in these *880* neighborhoods, and nearly three-quarters were either black or Hispanic.

By its very existence, the underclass *undermines* the precept that a rising economic tide lifts all boats.

Our report provides even more detail on the differences that divide minority groups, but the point is clear: minority life in America is not monolithic nor easily characterized by stereotypical thinking.

Hence, as we struggle in our workplaces and in the larger society with racial and ethnic diversity, we must recognize that within the superficial grouping of people by race or ethnic status, there is even further diversity of educational background, economic status and social standing.

Different problems faced by different groups require different solutons. There are no "one size fits all" programs to help minorities make their way in American society.

And of course, minority life in America is even more complex than portrayed by the Forum—as you well know. Californians will be the first to appreciate that in focusing on blacks and Hispanics, the Forum ignored one of the fastest-growing ethnic groups: Asian-Americans.

But we *did* examine the experience of *90 percent* of American minorities, and found that *two-thirds* of them are living at or below the margin. Many live in conditions of genuine human misery. Others are being left behind.

If our nation is to face the challenge of global economic competition, we clearly cannot write off *two-thirds* of our minorities, particularly when minorities are the fastest-growing segment of our population. To do so would be both economically foolish and morally wrong.

That leaves to our nation the challenge of defining an agenda to draw minorities into the economic mainstream. There are many tools available to help us meet this challenge. However, one tool available to help us meet this challenge. However, one tool is essential to improve the prospects of *all* minorities in America. And that common denominator is education.

Education may not be a sufficient condition to lift the desperate out of the underclass, or to ensure that those at the margin ultimately make it. But without it, there is not hope.

There is widespread agreement that our education system is not serving the nation well, particularly when it comes to teaching minorities. In just the past ten years, education reform has attracted more attention than perhaps any other social issue in this country.

And it has definitely invited more prescriptions for change. Hundreds of reports on education reform include literally thousands of proposals to improve our schools.

A few years ago, when the Forum was addressing issues of education and training reform, we consulted more than 20 major studies, which included more than 285 recommendations. Of those 285 proposals, we found only nine enjoyed the support of more than five reports. More important, over 70 percent of the specific recommendations had only a *single champion* behind them.

As we wrote at the time, "It is little wonder that progress in raising student achievement has been much too slow: As different pilots seize the helm of educational reform, the ship goes round in circles."

Thus, despite the outpouring of proposals for reform, little has truly been done. Given all the discussion, the multitude of reports, given all the speeches and similar leadership pronouncements, why has so little progress been made?

The Forum is currently in the midst of a long-term project intended to answer the question. We are working with the Public Agenda Foundation, an organization headed by pollster Dan Yankelovich, on a very intense public-education campaign to explore—and then to overcome—the obstacles to education reform.

We have two objectives. First, we want to understand why progress has been so sparing and so slow. Second, we hope to help fashion community-based consensus that will help localities around the United States get on with the business of strenthening the education of American students and the skills of American workers. We want to identify the obstacles—and then eliminate them.

As a prelude to our public-education campaigns, we conducted extensive public opinion research to identify common views on education among the American public. We found some surprising results and identified several important hurdles that stand between proposals for education reform and actual results.

We discovered that the most vocal proponents of education reform—the education associations, business groups, government agencies and think tanks—do not have much of the public behind them. In fact, the views of these groups, and more importantly, their remedies for our nation's educational problems, differ in startling ways from the views of the public.

We found, for instance, that the public believes values are the root of the problems in our schools. The problem plaguing schools, they say, is not low teacher pay, or excess overhead, or lack of choice, or the absence of school-based management. Instead, classrooms lack discipline. A high school diploma represents nothing more than a student having put in his or her time.

In other words, our schools are in trouble because of moral failings. A participant in one of our focus groups said that "the U.S. isn't like Japan. They are more studious over there. American kids are just interested in rock music, sneakers, and jeans." Another states that: "Our kids have no respect for teachers. They need more discipline."

This reasoning suggests that the public believed that in large measure our educational system is sound. Curriculum is not a major problem, teacher pay is not an issue, and science and math training is not necessarily deficient. On balance, the public says, educational opportunity exists—at least for the hard-working.

Individuals simply are not exploiting the opportunities available. In other words, American students and workers *could* have the skills needed to succeed in the workplace. They simply *choose* not to.

This discrepancy shows up in even more specific issues related to education. For example, because technology is important to our economic competitveness, numerous education reports have proposed additional science and math training, particularly for minorities, to ensure an ample supply of scientists and engineers.

But one of our focus group participants recommended a different solution. He said students "should work with slide rules."

This is not an extreme opinion, but an honest expression of a very common view that laziness or indifference to hard work lies at the heart of our educational deficiencies.

Our public opinion research unveiled some other findings that are particularly disturbing for those seeking to improve opportunities for the two-thirds of America's minorities who live at or below the margin.

For example, we found that America's minorities who live at or below the magin.

For example, we found that Americans remain deeply mistrustful of programs that appear to be a reincarnation of the "Great Society" days of LBJ. When experts call for higher funding for programs with excellent track records, such as Head Start, the public often views the proposal as another futile attempt to throw money at a problem.

After all, if the proposal is supposed to work today, it would have worked in the 1960s and the problem would have been solved by now.

The public also tends to believe that only K-through-12 counts. In other words, the public believes that preparing a competitive workforce can be achieved only by focusing on the "3R's."

Thus, the public is not generally receptive to the calls of experts for advanced skills training, adult literacy efforts and lifelong learning. That finding has major implications for all of you involved in *workplace-based* education and training.

And it bodes particularly harshly for those at risk of seeing their jobs eliminated by a plant relocation or the migration of jobs offshore. Other opportunities may be available for the dislocated, but without proper training and a solid foundation of skills, most decent jobs will remain beyond the grasp of those at or below the margin.

We are using our research results to guide our public-education campa igns. Our objective is not to prove the public wrong—for the simple reason that the public is not wrong.

Instead, there is a massive gap between *public opinion* and *expert opinion* that serves as a stumbling block to addressing real human resource problems such as high dropout rates, poor math and science skills, and inadequate preparation for school among the poor and many minorities.

That is why the Forum is attempting to broker information between community leaders and the public. Our goal is to help experts and special interests transcend their often-parochial concerns by understanding the sentiments of the public—and to encourage the public to consider choices for education reform other than simply prescribing harder work for their fellow citizens.

We hope to forge a compromise between the American people and the groups preparing the reports and proposing the solutions—by alerting both sides to the concerns of the other.

It is a question of leadership, a role that the Forum's corporate and university members are uniquely qualified to play. In the *Three Realities* report, Forum members spelled out not only what public policymakers should do to improve the conditions of minorities in America, they described changes that *they*, as private-sector leaders, must make in their own institutions.

Now, to follow up on our research about the public-expert gaps on school reform, Forum members will be hosting intensive public-education campaigns in cities across the country—from Hartford to Seattle.

In each city we will conduct intensive, six-week campaigns that will include comprehensive and repetitive media discussions of educational issues. Information will be conveyed to the public through a television documentary, newspaper articles, radio and TV talk shows, town meetings and similar activities that will engage the citizens of these communities in the education reform debate.

Each city's major TV station, newspaper, radio station, as well as civic, higher education and business leaders have agreed to participate in the project. And each campaign will culminate in a public vote on possible education reform options.

Leadership also requires being honest with the public. Our campaigns won't pull any punches when it comes to describing the costs of these reform options. We will lay out the costs of each choice—and we will be specific about the tradeoffs, or the consequences, of each option.

But in discussing costs, the Forum members have been persuaded by the Pay Now or Pay Later argument. As the *Three Realities* report points out, for instance, it costs $2,500 to provide Head Start or day care for the child of a working mother, but $7,300 to provide AFDC, food stamps and heating assistance for a mother of two who cannot work because of her child-care responsibilities. And it costs $600 to provide a year compensatory education, but $2,400 to have a child repeat a grade.

Our effort to build consensus should energize attempts to improve our learning systems. The past eight years of reporting on what should be done—beginning with the landmark report *A Nation At Risk*—reveals that little *can* be done absent broad agreement among the many participants in our education system—including teachers and business leaders, taxpayers and parents.

And although finding a common ground on education will benefit our entire society, perhaps no one will benefit more than the millions of minorities who lack the skills and training to realize the American Dream. The *Three Realities* report shows that minorities *can* make it in America.

If we can find ways to ensure that all minority citizens receive a sound education before they enter the workplace, others should be able to rise from the ranks of the working poor or the just-plain impoverished, too. And if our education system does its job when America's future workers are young, your job of managing diversity will be that much easier.

This, then, is the unfinished agenda.

Perhaps our greatest adversary in this effort is the "know-nothings." Some still see diversity as a problem—as a source of eternal and bitter conflict. A recent article in one of America's leading weekly magazines asserted that "a truly multiracial society will undoubtedly prove much harder to govern." That is a statement I reject.

Our nation has always been the melting pot. To our credit, we have found ways to reconcile differences among groups, when those same differences served as a source of unending conflict in other societies.

That is because, at heart, Americans are united by a common love of freedom, a vision of a better future, a presumption that all citizens deserve to be judged by the content of their character, not the color of their skin, and a belief that our economic system provides opportunities for the vast majority to prosper. Those values are nearly universal.

But conflict certainly *will* occur if American minorities can do no more than watch others do well. And that remains the condition of two-thirds of minorities in American life. The activities of the Forum will contribute in a modest way to offering minorities a greater stake in the nation's future. With the help of you and other concerned citizens, we can disprove the know-nothings, and we can do better than manage our diversity. We can continue to thrive, and create out of the many—one nation indivisible.

Thank you, and I wish you a successful conference.

III. RESTRUCTURING THE SCHOOLS: EQUITABLE FINANCING AND CHOICE

EDITOR'S INTRODUCTION

By 1990 the terms "equitable financing" and "choice" had entered the vocabulary of those concerned with education reform and, more specifically, with the restructuring of the schools. In the first of the articles in this section, Peter Hong writing in *Business Week* discusses the disparities between the annual budgets of school districts within the same state and the recent initiatives to even out such imbalances. School budgets are determined in large part by the tax base of the local communities, so that rich and poor districts may exist almost side by side. But state funding also enters in, and in a recent Texas Supreme Court case, the court citing "glaring disparities" in funding ordered the state legislature to make up the difference between the state's wealthiest and poorest school districts. As Hong points out, litigation of a related nature is in progress in other states as well.

The question of choice in schools that students attend has become even more an issue of the moment. In an article in *Time*, Walter Shapiro discusses the origins of the choice concept, which was originally known as the "voucher" system, for the tax vouchers that could be cashed in at any state-certified school. Now, public, private, and perhaps even parochial schools would all compete in a free marketplace in which the best would succeed and the worst managed would go under. The idea of the voucher system, popularized in the 1960s by the economist Milton Friedman, was advocated by President Reagan and is now advanced by President Bush, using the term "choice." As Shapiro notes, the hour seems to have come for a national experiment, since versions of it have already been initiated in some of the states.

In the final article, Evans Clinchy, writing in *Phi Delta Kappan* applauds the country's new interest in choice in schools, but warns against hasty, ill-conceived implementation. He concludes that the successful choice program must be restricted to public schools and must be racially and socially equitable.

THE MONEY QUESTIONS
THAT HAVE SCHOOLS STUMPED[1]

"Anything you can imagine, I need," says James Vasquez, superintendent of the Edgewood independent school district in San Antonio. In this low-income, largely Hispanic district, teachers often dig into their own pockets to pay for basic supplies. Many classrooms are not air-conditioned, and temperatures can soar above 100F in the Texas heat. High school students share a few 10-year-old computers.

Vasquez says such conditions reflect the best he can do on an annual budget of $3,150 per student, which covers free lunches for 92% of Edgewood's students plus teachers, books, and maintenance. In contrast, upper-middle-class Clear Lake High near Houston has two libraries and science lab areas, three gymnasiums, a pool, and dozens of new computers. Clear Lake's district tax base will generate $4,100 per student this year—and locals recently passed a $22 million bond issue to build new school facilities.

Lake year, the Texas Supreme Court ordered the state legislature to help even out such imbalances. But [then] Governor William P. Clements Jr. has twice rejected a proposed sales tax increase to raise $555 million for the schools. And Texas is but one example. Around the nation, hard questions—how to pay for public schools, how much to spend, and how to spend fairly—are being raised. But the drive for spending equality is hitting potholes of opposition: foes of higher taxes and those who resent dumping more money into the schools at a time when school quality and management are under sharp attack.

As in Texas, Kentucky and Montana courts have ruled recently against funding systems in which schools rely heavily on local property taxes. Similar suits are pending in a dozen other states. Indeed, funding disparities among school districts are near-universal.

The Edgewood schools first sued for equalization 22 years ago, in a case that went to the U.S. Supreme Court in 1973. Al-

[1]Article by Peter Hong. Reprinted from the June 4, 1990 issue of *Business Week* by special permission, copyright © 1990 by *McGraw-Hill, Inc.*

though the court ruled that spending differences do not violate the equal protection clause of the U.S. Constitution, it left open the possibility that they might defy state constitutions. A number of state courts have since overturned existing funding plans. Since the 1970s, the share of education spending funded by local property taxes has slipped to about 40% in most states, while state funding has crept to 50% or higher. Federal spending, mainly on programs for children with special needs, accounts for less than 10%.

These averages, however, mask a crazy quilt of state spending formulas. Hawaii's school system spent $4,500 on every pupil last year, paid for solely by sales and income taxes. Other states guarantee minimum budgets by district or per student, over and above what property taxes are able to raise. Some fund the gaps by pooling local property levies while others do so with various other taxes, lotteries, and spending caps.

Angry Voters. But many of these funding arrangements have become inadequate over time, as enrollments, community needs, and resources have changed. School districts in inner cities and the farm belt have seen their property-tax bases shrivel. In many states, competing needs are shrinking the dollars available for schools. In New Jersey, where recent state funding cuts have increased local tax burdens, voters angrily rejected proposed school budget hikes in April. Meanwhile, tax windfalls from corporate relocations and giant shopping centers have made some suburban districts dizzyingly wealthy.

A look at California shows just how rusty a funding formula can become. In 1978, California began equalizing school spending by increasing state funds to some school districts while holding others constant over time. But officials say that state allocations haven't kept pace with rising costs in poor districts where the school population has grown rapidly.

Now, the funding debate is being waged in a new context: the school reform movement. Since the early 1980s, the goal of improving education has taken precedence over that of equalizing resources. But pay raises for teachers, smaller class sizes, tougher graduation standards, and other recent reform efforts—along with a 30% growth in school budgets—have failed to improve achievement or lower drop-out rates. U.S students still perform worse than those in other industrial countries, despite one of the highest levels of national education spending.

Now, many experts are declaring that only total restructuring will fix the schools. "No matter how much money we distribute, even on an absolutely equitable basis, unless we fundamentally change the way we educate our children, it doesn't really matter," noted American Federation of Teachers President Albert Shanker in a recent speech.

Still, more money, carefully spent, probably could make a difference to some poor schools. Edgewood can afford to pay its teachers a starting salary of only $18,500, which trails wealthier Texas districts by as much as $7,000 and contributes to an annual teacher turnover of 20%.

Troubled schools may need more than their equal share of funds. To "equalize educational outcomes," says University of Colorado education finance expert C. Kent McGuire, "a good school-finance system would have a way to measure differences in need as well as ability to pay." Increasingly, states have attempted to do this.

But doubts have arisen about the education establishment's competence to spend intelligently. There's growing resistance to spending more on large school bureaucracies, for instance, or on bad teachers who are often difficult to fire.

Moreover, added spending in a school doesn't guarantee improved performance. Reviewing dozens of studies done over 20 years, Eric Hanushek of the University of Rochester has concluded in a controversial report that neither smaller classes, better facilities, higher teacher pay, nor more teacher training consistently yielded educational gains. In his recent study of New Jersey schools, Herbert J. Walberg, a professor of education at the University of Illinois at Chicago, found that students' backgrounds accounted for most of the achievement differentials from one district to another. Class differences are seen in the degree of parental involvement and expectations, which have a clear impact, he says.

Less Is More. Hudson Institute researcher Lewis J. Perelman argues that many rich schools could spend less and get more. He suggests that better use of technology can slash the cost of education by making it more efficient. For instance, two small classes in rural districts 100 miles apart could share a calculus teacher, using two-way videos.

The problem, as Perelman notes, is that equalization usually means raising the budgets of poor districts to those of the highest, without reference to whether wealthy districts are more efficient. "No one wants to give anything up," he says.

There is a constructive way out: Overhaul the educational system itself so that voters won't feel their money is being squandered. Kentucky took this route last year, when the state supreme court ordered the legislature to equalize school funding and also to reinvent the schools. Kentucky's General Assembly rose to the challenge, enacting a sweeping school reform law.

The law raises average school spending to about $3,000 per pupil. To help the poorer districts, it hikes state corporate income and sales taxes by 1%, mandates local taxation levels, and eliminates Kentucky's state income tax deduction for federal taxes paid. It offers bonuses to districts that markedly improve performance. And it slashes bureaucracy: All 500 jobs at the state education department will be reviewed, district hiring power will be curtailed, and local schools will control curriculum.

A new education commissioner can take over schools that fail to perform. "There's no question that without adequate money, [educating children] can't be done. But it takes a heck of a lot more than money," says former Kentucky Governor Bert T. Combs, now a lawyer who brought the school financing case. In the end, what citizens are willing to spend on the schools will depend on the quality of those institutions.

PICK A SCHOOL, ANY SCHOOL[2]

It is a hot summer day on Maple Street. See Dick and Jane play Nintendo. See Mommy and Daddy turn off the switch. Whine, Dick, whine! Pout, Jane, pout!

"Today is a very special day," explains Mommy. "You get to pick your school."

The family drives to a big school of red brick. "This was where I went," says Daddy proudly. "In olden days, they made kids go here. But you, Dick and Jane, are so very lucky. You can choose."

[2]Reprint of an article by Walter Shapiro for *Time*. *Time* S 3 '90. 136:70, 72. Copyright 1990 The Time Inc. Magazine Company. Reprinted with permission.

A nice teacher with a big smile greets them. She uses large words like achievement and learning modalities. Then she tells Dick and Jane about important stuff. "You could have hot dogs or hamburgers every day for lunch," she says.

The next school is made of stone and surrounded by pretty trees and grass. "This was my school," says Mommy proudly. "It cost your grandparents lots of money to send me here. But it was worth it."

"Do we have the money?" ask Dick and Jane eagerly.

"You don't have to be rich to go here anymore," says Mommy. "These days, the government gives everyone money to go to any school they like."

"Oh, goody!" shout Dick and Jane.

The notion of freely choosing between public and private schools may no longer be just a Dick-and-Jane fable. Next week more than 400 students from Milwaukee's inner city will begin attending private neighborhood academies with the aid of $2,500 grants from the state of Wisconsin. In November, Oregon will vote on a landmark initiative that would give parents as much as a $2,500 tuition tax credit for each child in a private or religiously affiliated school. Already, students statewide in Minnesota as well as in such widely praised individual school districts as Cambridge, Mass., and New York City's East Harlem can select which public schools they will attend. These are grassroots manifestations of a political idea that is rapidly gaining momentum and, if fully implemented, holds the potential to radically transform American public education.

• In September 400 inner-city Milwaukee students will enter private schools with $2,500 grants from the state of Wisconsin

• In November Oregon will vote on an initiative that would give parents up to $2,500 in tuition tax credit for each child in private school

• Excessive bureaucracy leads to inflated public-education costs: spending per pupil averages $4,590 in public schools compared to $2,690 for Catholic secondary schools

Originally known as the "voucher system" and now often referred to under the innocuous shorthand of "choice," the theoretical concept is daringly simple. Instead of funding and administering public schools through stifling bureaucracies, government would provide tuition vouchers for every student. These could be cashed in at any state-certified school—public, private or perhaps even parochial. Ideally, the result would be that schools of all kinds—both old and new—would jostle and compete in the free marketplace.

The winners would be those schools that attract a full enrollment of students, probably through innovative programs or a demonstrated record of academic success. But the real victors would be children of the poor and the hard-pressed urban middle class, who now have no alternative other than attending their crumbling local public school. And if some publicly run schools fail to compete successfully, they would go out of business. A brutal system perhaps, but one guaranteed to shake the torpor out of American education.

The battle over educational vouchers blurs ideological lines by pitting theorists of the right and the left against cautious centrist reformers and the custodians of the educational status quo. The idea was popularized by economist Milton Friedman in his 1962 conservative classic, *Capitalism and Freedom*. Liberal activists then gave the notion a brief vogue in the early 1970s as an experiment sponsored by the Office of Economic Opportunity. The Reagan Administration tepidly tried to revive vouchers in the mid-1980s, and George Bush gave lip service to the concept during the 1988 campaign. But the current intellectual momentum stems from the publication of *Politics, Markets, and America's Schools* by political scientists John Chubb and Terry Moe. This influential book bears the imprimatur of the Brookings Institution, Washington's leading liberal think tank.

At first glance, the book seems unlikely to send anyone to the educational barricades. It is a laborious statistical analysis of the crisis in public education. But in their final two chapters, Chubb and Moe suddenly transform themselves into radical deconstructionists. They theorize that "excessive bureaucratization and centralization are no historical accident . . . They are inevitable consequences of America's institutions of democratic control." The more political pressure is exerted to improve the schools, they argue, the more bureaucracy is created to monitor the new reform nostrums. In their view, only a choice system that frees the schools from political pressures entirely—and introduces the competition of the marketplace—can make a lasting difference.

The most controversial aspect of any voucher plan (a term that Chubb and Moe avoid because of its Friedmanesque heritage) is the idea of permitting private and even parochial schools to compete with public institutions. But Chubb insists that choice plans that allow open enrollment only within the public-school system will not provide enough competition or sufficient diversity. "Public-school choice," he argues, "is merely a demand-side test. There's no change on the supply side."

Under a full-fledged voucher system, private institutions would spring up to cater to the needs of parents who demand better education. The vouchers would, in theory, provide roughly the same amount of money as it now costs to educate each student in the public schools; in some over-bureaucratized systems like New York City's, that is more than $5,500 a year, higher than the tuition at some private schools. Government would still have a role: private schools, as they do today, would have to abide by state certification standards and could not racially discriminate. Chubb and Moe also suggest that there could be extra financial incentives to encourage schools to accept problem students. Thus even potential dropouts would have an alternative to their local P.S. 99.

Critics argue that adoption of voucher plans would sound the death knell of the public school as a democratic institution that melds children from all classes, backgrounds and races in a modern-day melting pot. In truth, that pluralistic dream died years ago in most districts. Today 63% of all black students attend predominantly nonwhite schools. Public education is also increasingly economically segregated. A voucher system may not foster the ethnic diversity of a Benetton ad, but by diluting the distinction between public and private schools, it would add much needed equality to American education.

The harshest attacks against Chubb and Moe have come from some of the educators most sympathetic to incremental reform. "Their book is a profound example of the intellectual community's abandoning our most important democratic institution," claims Bill Honig, the California superintendent of public instruction. The choice model of rewarding schools for attracting students rather than successfully educating them troubles Albert Shanker, the president of the American Federation of Teachers. "If your goal is merely to recruit students," Shanker says, "you can do that by offering a trip to Disneyland or with a good football team."

The debate over educational vouchers can be seen as a symptom of America's loss of faith in liberal government itself, for public schools have always been the collective institution most closely monitored by the people. If, as Chubb and Moe argue, a free market is the only antidote to educational bureaucracy, then virtually all government programs, save tax collection, are implicitly called into question. Yet the crisis in the schools is so severe that vouchers must be seriously considered, which is why Dick and Jane seem well on their way toward becoming free-market conservatives.

PUBLIC SCHOOL CHOICE: ABSOLUTELY NECESSARY BUT NOT WHOLLY SUFFICIENT[3]

Twenty years ago it was a wild and crazy idea. Today, public school choice is rapidly becoming the latest tidal wave in an ocean of public school reform. School districts across the country are instituting choice in a variety of *intra*district forms, ranging from a few magnet schools to entire school systems. Moreover, such states as Minnesota have instituted laws permitting *inter*district choice—allowing students and parents to choose to attend schools in other school districts and to take courses in public colleges and universities for dual credit.

George Bush, seeking to become the "Education President," has declared public school choice to be "a national necessity." He appears poised to make choice the educational centerpiece of his Administration and thus *the* school reform of the 1990s.

For those of us who began to wonder seriously about the possibilities of choice two decades ago, the burgeoning success of this idea is heartwarming. Especially pleasing is the fact that the movement now appears limited to choice among *public* schools and public schools *only*. Apparently we have managed—at least

[3]Reprint of a speech by Evans Clinchy, Senior Field Associate, Institute for Responsive Education. *Phi Delta Kappa, D '89. 71: 289–294. Copyright © 1989 by Phi Delta Kappan.* Reprinted by permission of author.

for the moment—to put to rest vouchers, tuition tax credits, and other forms of nonpublic school choice that would harm the national effort to improve public education. While all this success may warm our hearts, it is just a bit frightening to some of us.

Why frightening? First, we see many states and school systems riding the tidal wave of choice with little thought and virtually no planning. Choice instituted in a hasty, ill-conceived fashion can easily turn out to be—and in all too many cases is turning out to be—no choice at all: a charade and even a hoax, a pseudo-innovation that produces no significant change in the old authoritarian school system that adopts a choice plan. A new plan may seem to present genuine alternatives when in fact it is offering only a few minor variations on the theme of the standard, traditional school.

Second, we are frightened because we see a danger that choice may be oversold as a magical solution to *all* the problems that afflict our public schools—a possibility for which those of us who have enthusiastically (and perhaps indiscriminately) promoted choice for so long are no doubt partly responsible. If this happens and choice does *not* produce the expected magical cures, then the resulting disappointment could turn everyone against the whole idea.

WHY CHOICE IS NECESSARY

Worried though some of us may be, I do not know of a single one of us who would question the basic notion that empowering parents to specify and then to choose the different kinds of public schooling that they want for their children is absolutely necessary if our public schools are to improve. Nor would we restrict empowerment to parents. Professional practitioners, our teachers and principals, must also be empowered to specify and then to put into practice the various kinds of schooling that they believe are best for their students.

Above and beyond these obvious virtues, both parental choice and professional choice, when properly conceived and executed, are necessary *because they turn our traditional authoritarian system of public education upside down*. And this shakeup is genuine change, real reform, true restructuring.

Our traditional system, the one that is gradually changing into something quite different, has attempted at every turn to hold parents, students, and professional educators hostage. It has taken for granted that it has both the right and the duty to tell its clients where and when to go to school; what the educational philosophy, the curriculum, and the organization of that school will be; who can and cannot teach there; whether the children are succeeding or failing in that school; and whether those children can graduate from that school and go on to the next level of schooling designated by the system.

That same system has told its teachers and principals where they can and cannot work, what they will teach and how they will teach it, how the school will be organized and operated, how the students will be judged and graded, how the professionals themselves will be evaluated, and how they will be rewarded financially.

Choice is changing all of that. At least choice has the potential to change all of that if it is properly understood, carefully though through, and implemented in gradual stages, with no stage begun until the previous stage is successfully in place.

THE REQUIREMENTS OF CHOICE

A considerable measure of care in implementing choice plans is necessary because choice clearly implies and requires *but in no way automatically guarantees* two profound alterations in the way the present system operates.

First, choice requires that we abandon our cherished notion that there can be a single, all-inclusive definition of "educational excellence": a single, standardized approach to schooling; a single, canonized, culturally literate curriculum; and a single way of organizing and operating a school that is suitable for all students and serves all students equally well. Quite the opposite. We need genuine diversity in our approaches to schooling, creating different kinds of schools to serve our diverse student population and to accommodate the range of parental and professional beliefs about what public education should be and do.

As Howard Gardner, a professor of developmental psychology at Harvard University, has put it:

The single most important contribution education can make to a child's development is to help him toward a field where his talents best suit him, where he will be satisfied and competent. We've completely lost sight of that. Instead, we subject everyone to an education where, if you succeed, you will be best suited to be a college professor. And we evaluate everyone according to whether they meet that narrow standard of success.

We should spend less time ranking children and more time helping them to identify their natural competencies and gifts and cultivate those. There are hundreds of ways to succeed and many, many different abilities that will help you get there.

"Genuine" diversity means just that: a range of educational options that extends from preschool through high school and that encompasses everything from a very traditional "back-to-basics" approach, through such modest departures from the norm as "continuous progress" or "individually guided" education, to such truly radical types of schooling as Montessori, "open," or even "microsociety" schools. We also need more schools that specialize in particular aspects of the intellectual and artistic worlds, schools that offer interested students a chance to develop their talents in the fine and performing arts, in science and technology, or in the humanities.

As Mary Anne Raywid, one of the pioneers in the field of public school choice, has aptly put it:

Clearly, we must call a halt to our century-long march toward standardization. We must forget such fruitless battles as whether or not to begin all reading instruction with phonics and seek instead to match our teaching strategies to particular students—starting some youngsters with phonics and others with drastically different approaches. The evidence supporting such a strategy is extensive, varied, and certainly not new; we know for a fact that different youngsters learn in different ways and according to different patterns. When we persist in imposing a single instructional approach on all children, we succeed with some students and systematically handicap others. There is no reason (beyond our own perversity) to continue to assume that some single "right" approach exists that will suit every student.

Seymour Fliegel, another of the champions of choice and formerly deputy superintendent in Community School District No. 4 in East Harlem, has described how that district has actively sought to provide the kind of diversity Raywid advocates:

The aim here has been to create a system that—instead of trying to fit students into some standardized school—has a school to fit *every* student in this district. No one gets left out; no one gets lost. Every kid is important; every kid can learn if you put him or her in the right environment. But since kids have this huge range of different needs, different interests, and different ways of learning, we've got to have a wide diversity of schools. Which is what, after 13 years at it, we've just about got.

This truly diverse range of approaches to schooling is precisely what many of the school systems riding the crest of the wave of choice are *not* providing. All too often, the local school board and the central administrators of a school system will make a great show of instituting a choice plan, either for purposes of peaceful desegregation or because parents and professionals are demanding it. In many cases, however, the decisions as to what choices the school system will offer are made by the school board and (still more likely) the central administration. With a few notable exceptions, neither parents nor teachers and principals have been involved in making these decisions.

In only a few cases (e.g., Indianapolis and three districts in Massachusetts—Worcester, Lowell, and Fall River) have parents been asked to describe the different kinds of schooling that they want for their children. In these school systems, all parents of children in the public elementary and junior high schools were given a list of choices and asked to select the ones they believed would provide their children with the educational excellence that all parents seek.

In Worcester, Lowell, and Fall River, the range of options contained in the parent surveys was determined not by the central administration buy by citywide parent councils representing the parents of every school in the city. And in Fliegel's East Harlem district, the "alternative concept" schools were created by teachers who were encouraged to step forward and describe to the district administrators the different kinds of schools that they had always dreamed of working in. The district helped the teachers to establish their dream schools and helped the parents and students to choose among them.

But active participation by clients and practitioners in the decision-making process is not the norm. Moreover, even when parents are asked what they want, the school systems do not necessarily go on to create the schools that parents request. In Lowell, for example, the two schools most desired by parents were a K-8 school for the fine and performing arts and a K-8 microsociety school. These options were provided in the form of brand-new schools that draw students from all over the city (which is often the only solution to the problem of creating truly diverse and unusual schools). In Worcester, on the other hand, parents have asked for a Montessori school, an open or developmental school, and a microsociety school. However, these options have not been created.

A second—and also rarely successful—approach to the creation of diversity in the public schools is for the school system simply to allow each existing school to devise its own "distinctive" or "magnet" program. Since the parents and students in such existing schools are there because they happen to live in the school's attendance area, and since the teachers are there for the most part because they happened to be at the top of a list when a vacancy occurred in that particular school, there is little reason to hope that such a motley assortment of people (none of them there by real choice) could ever agree on anything but a minor variation on the traditional school. As one parent in Boston recently put it, "If you give me a choice of five or 10 or 20 schools that are all just about the same and if they're all mediocre and not what I want anyway, what kind of a choice is that?"

Indeed, the power of parental and professional choice is (or should be) precisely the fact that there can be a genuinely diverse range of schools that parents and teachers want, *because no one is forced* to be in a school that they do not want to be in. *Everyone* in a true school of choice has freely chosen that school. The staff and the students are there because they all agree on the educational approach they want, including the educational philosophy of the school, what its curriculum should be, and how it should be organized and run.

Given this situation, everyone in the school shares a sense of the school's mission. Parents, students, teachers, and administrators can buckle down to the task of making the school a truly excellent example of its particular approach to public education. In schools that do not have such a shared mission, conflicts and disagreements almost inevitably produce unhappiness, low morale, apathy, and—finally—the mediocrity we all deplore. In short, choice without genuine diversity is no choice at all.

THE NEED FOR AUTONOMY

The second great alteration is our traditional way of organizing a school system that is clearly required—*but not guaranteed*—by choice is the bestowal of *autonomy* on individual schools. Once a system of truly diverse schools has been created, each one of them should be given the power to determine its educational philosophy, its curriculum, and its organization and governance structure; to choose its teaching and administrative staff; and to set its own spending priorities.

This powerful idea (often called "school-based" or "school-site" management) is currently being espoused by many educational thinkers, most notably Albert Shanker, president of the American Federation of Teachers; Joe Nathan and Ted Kolderie of the Hubert H. Humphrey Institute of Public Affairs at the University of Minnesota; members of the Task Force on Teaching as a Profession of the Carnegie Forum on Education and the Economy (in that group's 1986 report, *A Nation Prepared: Teachers for the 21st Century*); and members of the National Governors' Association (in their 1986 report, *Time for Results: The Governors' 1991 Report*).

Even in terms of such a simplistic measure of success as student achievement, the empowerment of individual schools appears to have yielded some remarkable results. Using data from a national study of 1,000 public and private high schools, John Chubb and Terry Moe of the Brookings Institution came to several provocative conclusions. One was that the most recent wave of school reform—the one that has emphasized mandates handed down from state governments and central offices of school systems—has produced and will continue to produce little or no real improvement in student performance. These mandates imposed from on high have called for stricter "academic standards," more homework, more testing, greater uniformity and standardization of curriculum and teaching methods, and increased control over what schools and teachers do.

When all their data were analyzed and such factors as student aptitude, minority/majority mix, family income, and money spent on the schools were controlled, the researchers concluded that the most crucial element of those schools in which student achievement was high was the effectiveness of the school's organization, defined as the school's freedom from higher-level administrative control. Given such freedom, the staff members and parents can create "a common school purpose" or "a shared view of education." The researchers concluded that, "all other things being equal, attendance at an effectively organized [high] school for four years is worth at least a full year of additional achievement over attendance at an ineffectively organized school."

THE THIRD NECESSITY

True diversity and genuine autonomy may be necessary for the achievement of both choice and educational excellence. However, neither of these good things should be instituted without an overriding concern for the third great necessity: educational equity for all students, especially poor and minority students and women.

Thus all forms of choice, be they within a district or between districts, must be carefully controlled to make sure that every parent and every child has an equal chance to benefit from the advantages that choice confers. How this goal can be achieved within school districts is exemplified in the Massachusetts districts of Cambridge, Lowell, and Fall River—districts in which *every* school is a magnet school or school of choice.

In each of these school systems, equity is provided through policies that guarantee equal access to (and thus the legal desegregation of) every school for all students. Each school has quotas of minority representation that are roughly comparable to the minority/majority mix of the public school population as a whole, and each school seeks to maintain about a 50/50 balance between males and females. Thus spaces are reserved in all schools for poor and minority students and for females. No school has academic or behaviorally selective admissions criteria; all schools are open to all students by parental choice within these equity guidelines.

Such controls do mean that choice cannot be absolute or totally unfettered. Constraints imposed by concerns about equity will mean that parents will not always get their first choice of school. However, if this situation occurs frequently, it probably means that the district either has failed to survey parents to find out how many of them want which kinds of schools or has failed to provide an adequate number of the schools parents do want.

Charles Glenn, executive director of the Office of Educational Equity for the Massachusetts Department of Education and one of the prime movers behind the push for choice *and* equity, has discussed the relationship between the two objectives:

It has become clear that choice can do much to promote equity. It does so by creating conditions which encourage schools to become more effective, it does so by allowing schools to specialize and thus to meet the needs of some students very well rather than all students at a level of minimum adequacy, and it does so by increasing the influence of parents over the education of their children in a way which is largely conflict free.

Thus we should pursue choice, by all means—but never choice that benefits primarily the already advantaged segments of our society and leaves poor and minority parents and students right where they have always been, behind society's eight ball.

THE ROLE OF CENTRAL ADMINISTRATION

Do the revolutionary changes described above render central administrators and local school boards irrelevant and unnecessary? Quite the contrary. Indeed, while the role of the central administration is turned upside down, its importance is diminished not one whit.

As Rhonda Schneider, then acting commissioner of the Massachusetts State Department of Education, explained in 1986:

> We have high expectations for *all* students, and we are convinced that the best education occurs when those nearest the student make the key decisions about how they will learn. That is why, over recent years, we have developed an extensive program of support for diversity among urban schools, providing parent choice on the basis of different approaches to education. . . .

> Our commitment in Massachusetts has been to make schools *different in focus but equal in quality* and to give all parents the opportunity and the information to make significant choices for their children. . . .

> In this process the role of central administration [and of the local school board] has been to orchestrate diversity, to insure that the common educational goals of the school system are met, even if in many different ways, and that no student is neglected in the process.

"To orchestrate diversity," a lovely phrase, eloquently expresses the crucial set of tasks that local school boards and central administrators are now called on to perform. First, they need to set the common educational goals for all schools and all students (but *not* the ways in which those goals will be met); second, they need to make sure that parents, older students, teachers, and principals all have played a role in making the decisions about the creation of a full range of diverse schools and can now freely choose the schools they want; third, they need to guarantee that poor and minority students and their parents are fully empowered to take advantage of everything that diversity and choice can offer them.

A NEW FRAMEWORK

It is tempting to believe that if we introduce diversity, choice, autonomy for individual schools, and strict equity controls, thereby turning the old system upside down, we will have done enough to insure that our local school systems will be able to provide genuine educational excellence. Would that it were so. As good and necessary as all these changes are, public school choice and its associated restructurings provide only a framework within which our chances of solving many seemingly intractable problems are improved.

This new framework, for instance, should make public schooling much more attractive to the creative people already working in our public school systems and to all such people who might be thinking about teaching as a career. As Mary Romer-Coleman, assistant director of alternative concept schools in New York's Community School District No. 4, has noted:

> [The fact that] we are able to treat teachers as adult professionals and give them a chance to do what they've always believed should be done . . . has helped prevent teacher burnout and kept many of the best teachers in our schools.
> I was a teacher here in District No. 4, and let me tell you I would have been long gone if I hadn't had a chance to work in the kind of school I believed in. And this is true, I think, for most of the teachers in the alternative concept schools. . . .

Choice does not guarantee that this increased satisfaction will come about, nor does it in any way guarantee that the deadwood in our systems (whether teachers, principals, or central administrators) will be quickly and easily replaced—or that the people taking their places will necessarily be convinced that the new school system required by diversity and choice should be immediately instituted.

Indeed, in all too many instances the policy of diversity and controlled choice has been installed as a citywide desegregation measure only to languish as the entrenched bureaucracy dreams up all sorts of ingenious reasons why it should not and will not work, why surveys of parents and teachers should not be conducted, why decision-making authority should not be transferred downward from the central bureaucracy to the induvidual school.

Even in Buffalo, New York, where we find one of the leading and most successful examples of what choice can do for a large urban school system, things do not change that rapidly. The attitudes of a handful of Buffalo schoolpeople have been forcefully characterized by Florence Baugh, a member and former president of the Buffalo Board of Education and a leader of the black community in that city:

Let me tell you what I think about you educators. . . . I'm talking about most educators, including many right here in Buffalo. I think you're the most staid, dyed-in-the-wool, dull, the most resistant-to-change people on earth. You know, we have procedures, ways things are done in the school system which have been done since Day One. I'll talk to some of our people about doing something differently, and I'll get the response, "But that's the way we've always done it." . . . It doesn't matter whether it has any merit. It doesn't matter if there's anything happening as a result of doing it this way other than protecting the way it's always been done.
I give this lecture to superintendents all the time. The schools are for children, not for the convenience of you staff folk. We could do all sorts of wonderful things in our school systems if only you educators weren't so inflexible.

THE ULTIMATE NECESSITY

Now it is true that a new system of public schooling based on diversity, choice, and empowerment for individual schools does not by itself cost a great deal more than the traditional system, since it is essentially a new and better way of spending the money we are currently spending. There *will be* extra costs involved in reorganizing the existing system, in creating the new schools that will be required to achieve true diversity, and in creating the parent information and support systems that we need. There are also some additional costs for transporting students. Even if these associated costs are minimal, that doesn't mean we can get a world-class system of public schools on the cheap.

While the new educational framework provided by diversity and choice may dramatically improve the public's satisfaction with its public schools and thus may make taxpayers more willing to invest in public education, there are simply too many other necessities that diversity and choice do not guarantee to provide. These include adequate salaries for teachers, better working conditions in schools (including adequate supplies, equipment, materials, and support services), and decent school facilities. We also need to provide vastly increased funding for our crumbling urban school systems and for all the additional educational, health, and social services that poor and minority children in those systems require if they are to break the cycle of poverty and disadvantage and to escape from the underclass.

It is becoming clear that we need early childhood education for all children and that we need to make radical changes in the education of teachers and administrators. Although diversity and choice do constitute an almost automatic, built-in system of educational research and development, we need a much more elaborate, better-organized, and better-funded system of support for genuine innovation and experimentation.

Just this partial list guarantees that we will have to spend a great deal more money on our public schools than we do now—at least twice as much. In these days of federal, state, and local budget deficits and consequent cutting of education budgets, such a statement may strike many readers as outlandish. If so, then I submit that those people have their heads (and their pocketbooks) in the educational sand. Throughout our history, this country has nickel-and-dimed public education and yet expected it to perform miracles. We have paid for a modest, utilitarian Model T and expected it to outperform a luxurious Dusenberg.

We still spend more of our gross national product (6.4% in 1988) on weapons and defense than on our entire system of public education from pre-school through college and university (4.5% in 1988). Surely these figures should be reversed. Just a single stealth bomber will cost at least half a billion dollars (not counting the inevitable cost overruns and the costs of fixing all the things that turn out not to work). That's more than the federal government currently puts into the creation of magnet schools ($413 million). A fleet of 100 such bombers would cost us at least $50 billion over the next decade or so, which is the minimum amount of money that should be added to the *federal* education budget every year in that same period.

What we need is a more civilized set of national priorities that could lead to a wiser and more humane (or kinder, gentler) American society. There is nothing stopping this country from having a superb system of public education—if we really want it. Do we?

IV. URBAN EDUCATION: THE WORST CASE SCENARIO

EDITOR'S INTRODUCTION

The final section of this compilation concerns itself with the state of large inner-city schools, whose student populations are made up largely of the poor and disadvantaged. The problems of these schools are staggering: in order for their educational mission to succeed it must overcome the apathy and the violence-and-drugs world of their students' ghetto surroundings. In the first of the articles in this section, Gene I. Maeroff, in an article from *Phi Delta Kappan*, writes of his visits across the U.S. to urban high schools, which have been bypassed by the reform movements of the 1980s. Characteristically, he found the schools to be large, impersonal places in which students lack a sense of belonging and see no relation between what they are asked to do in the classroom and the world that awaits them outside the school. Unsupported by homes in which education is encouraged and conditioned to have low expectations for themselves, students are demoralized and perform well below the national average.

Writing in *Newsweek*, Jonathan Kozol views these young people as outcasts in a rich society. Thirty percent of them, he notes, will drop out before finishing school, and many will remain functional illiterates. Melinda Beck, also writing in *Newsweek*, focuses on the Chicago school system, considered by many educators to be the nation's worst. Morale is so low that teachers as well as students are frequently absent. Ironically, one of the system's major problems was brought about by an effort to desegregate the schools in 1980, precipitating a "white flight" to the suburbs. Once half white, the student population is now 87 percent minority, many from families living at a poverty level. Roughly half of Chicago's public school students, Beck points out, drop out of school before graduation, and of those that remain only a third can read at or above the national average.

In contrast to Beck's picture of a seemingly hopeless situation, Warren Chapman, in an article in *Phi Delta Kappan* written three years later, offers a more positive view. Chapman discusses a major program underway by the Illinois State Board of Education to help at-risk children. Through state-sponsored grants, pilot projects involving parents more closely in an effort to raise students' test scores have demonstrated successful outcomes. A final article by Jerry Buckley in *U. S. News & World Report* describes a daring program for reform of urban schools in Rochester, New York, under which its teachers are paid among the highest salaries in the nation. The plan shifts much of the decision-making to teachers and administrators in individual schools, while making them more accountable for student performance. The undertaking was the outcome partly of an effort by Rochester's business community, including the mammoth Kodak company, to commit its financial resources and management skills to the city's ailing school system. Conceived as a 10-year experiment, and widely regarded as a model for the country, the program bears close watching.

WITHERED HOPES, STILLBORN DREAMS[1]

No white suburb in America would long tolerate the low academic achievement taken for granted in urban high schools attended largely by blacks and Hispanics. In big city after big city, minority students by the tens of thousands leave school each year—some as dropouts, some as graduates—utterly unprepared to participate in and contribute to a democratic society. They lack the skills that will allow them to obtain gainful employment, and they are devoid of the preparation that will lead to success in further education. They are what the Carnegie Council on Policy Studies warned almost a generation ago could become the nation's "lumpen proletariat."

A reform movement that was supposed to improve public education has been largely irrelevant to the needs of urban minority students. The reforms have either totally bypassed big-city school

[1]Reprint of an article by Gene I. Maeroff, a senior fellow at the Carnegie Foundation for the Advancement of Teaching. Reprinted by permission of *Phi Delta Kappan*, 69: 633-8. My '88. Copyright © 1988 by *Phil Delta Kappan*. Reprinted with permission of author.

districts or have produced changes that lengthened the time for instruction or raised requirements for diplomas without addressing the underlying circumstances that lead to failure for these students.

My visits to urban high schools across the country showed them to be large, impersonal places in which students lack a sense of belonging and see no connection between what they are asked to do in the classroom and the world that awaits them outside the school. I found the atmosphere in such schools often unsupportive of education and the demands and expectations low. Students say that they are unmotivated and that they see no reason to attend school, except that there is little else to do with their time.

Attendance is atrocious, and statistics that show students marked present at the beginning of the day do not reflect the degree to which individual classes are cut. There is in urban high schools throughout the country what the Chicago Panel on Public School Policy and Finance described as "a widespread 'culture of cutting.'" What passes as work in many courses is embarrassingly simple, and the level of discussion and the papers written by students (mostly in class, because few do any homework) are not truly on a high school level. Large-scale low achievement is accepted as the norm.

Readers can get a taste of the problem by looking in on a ninth-grade English class at a Chicago high school. During a composition lesson, the students were asked to write briefly about why they would choose a particular occupation. "We concentrate on the mechanics of writing so far as their second-, third-, and fourth-grade reading levels will allow," said the teacher. Indeed, the products of their labors, which lasted an entire period, very much resembled what might be produced in the lower grades of many suburban elementary schools. Wrote one student: "I would like to Be a judge and put Bad people in jail and judge make a lot of money to just like the foot ball player even More and I am glad that it is judges in the World to put the people in jail."

What is clearly needed is a fresh approach to urban education, involving smaller learning units and a different philosophy of instruction. The goal must be to create within each learning unit a sense of community and a desire on the part of students to belong to that community. Teachers must have fewer students and spend more time getting to know them. The curriculum must be narrower in scope—as it ought to be in all schools—so that students learn a few topics well, learning how to learn in the process, rather than trying to skim across a vast ocean of material. More classes must be organized around seminars, discussions, and cooperative learning, and students must be encouraged to take greater responsibility for their own education. Ideas and concepts, not facts and statistics, should form the core of this experience.

This reshaping of schools to better serve black students is a mission that America has historically been reluctant to accept. During the days of slavery, those in power acknowledged that laws prohibiting the education of blacks were intended to perpetuate "compulsory ignorance." Even five years after the Civil War, 90% of school-age blacks were not in school. As recently as 1940, public schools in the South operated on an average school year of 175 days for whites and 156 days for blacks, according to a report sponsored by the National Institute of Education.

"The notion that this nation once had good schools for the masses of African-American students but has since let them deteriorate is inaccurate," the National Alliance of Black School Educators stated in a 1984 report. "The institutionalization of deprivation and disenfranchisement among schools has permitted race and socioeconomic status to function as the chief determinants of access to quality treatment for children. The public schools often represent an integration of society's most crippling diseases—indifference, injustice, and inequity."

Schools in big cities must do more to lure poor minority youngsters into the mainstream by counteracting the isolation of their lives. Urban black students, in particular, are surrounded by failure, both in and out of school. Normally they see but few examples of success, except possibly in sports, entertainment, and illicit activities. Their sense of the future is stunted, and, unlike more advantaged youngsters, it does not include academic achievement in any way.

Hopes wither; dreams are stillborn. The isolation suffered by these students is underscored from the moment they enter school. A visit to an urban elementary school, the place where it all starts, will quickly bring home the reality of this isolation. Such a place is the Beethoven Elementary School on Chicago's depressed South Side, a school dwarfed by the Robert Taylor Homes, the huge housing project it faces—26 buildings in which 20,000 people live, mostly women and children on welfare.

The inner city has long been populated by poor people, but what makes the situation different today—and exacerbates the isolation—is the flight of middle-class blacks and the virtual abandonment of entire black neighborhoods to the poorest of the poor. There has been a bifurcation, described by Nicholas Lemann in *The Atlantic*, that has drained the ghettos of many of those who might be constructive role models for the young. A new kind of society is emerging in these neighborhoods, one with its own values, one that is "utterly different from that of the American mainstream." Education does not have a high priority in this setting.

Claude Brown and other commentators note the emergence of a black urban youth culture in which time in prison and unwed parenthood are the rituals of coming of age. *Time* called inner-city black males "America's newest lost generation," and the *Christian Science Monitor* called poor blacks the "exiles among us." William Julius Wilson wrote of neighborhoods in which "the chances are overwhelming that children will seldom interact on a sustained basis with people who are employed or with families that have a steady breadwinner . . . [where] the relationship between schooling and postschool employment takes on a different meaning."

The urban public schools, bequeathed to the impoverished, have an almost eerie aura about them, as though they were situated in one of the "homelands" to which blacks in South Africa have been confined. Despair reigns supreme among the young. "I don't have any goals," said a young male student in a Houston high school. "I live with my grandmother, and she tells me to do my schoolwork, but she can't read, so she can't help me. Nobody can help me."

Isolation of this sort strengthens the hold of the subculture, giving free play to values that neither reinforce schooling nor encourage the development of the habits of mind needed for academic success. Little happens in many schools or in many homes to build confidence in educational abilities. "They have been filled with so many stereotypes of low achievement that they tend to accept them," said the assistant principal of a high school in New Orleans. "Our goal must be to get students without a history of achievement to believe they can be successful."

Many students whose existence is rooted in urban poverty simply do not have the everyday experiences that might nurture their intellectual development and complement the mission of the school. "Some kids in this school just don't have anyone at home to say, 'I'm proud of you—keep up the good work,'" noted a student at a high school in Houston.

A sad result of their isolation is that many minority students, lagging hopelessly behind in academic achievement for their age, cannot appraise clearly the work they are doing and do not realize that it is not on the high school level. Frequently they do not possess a realistic understanding of just how badly they are lagging. They have no basis for drawing such academic comparisons, because they hardly ever come in contact with anyone other than similarly low-achieving students.

"I don't think I'm having too much trouble with reading," said a young woman at a high school in New Orleans. She was in the 10th grade and had a reading test score that placed her on the third-grade level. An 11th-grader at a high school in Los Angeles, who had not taken algebra or geometry and was currently enrolled in a course called "High School Mathematics," in which the class was learning to add mixed numbers, said: "I'll need this more than I'll need geometry and algebra in the world, and it'll help me more in life. I want to be an architect." He had little comprehension of the field to which he said he aspired, and even less knowledge of what is required to get there.

Many urban minority students have not the slightest clue of what it takes to attain academic goals. The climate in the schools they attend often bodes ill for achievement. Students routinely arrive after the bell has rung—perhaps a quarter of the class comes late—slamming the door behind them, one after the other; walking in front of the teacher; and repeatedly disrupting the lesson as if the teacher were doing nothing of consequence.

During lessons, teachers are frequently forced to compete for attention with unruly and disrespectful students. A world history teacher in a Chicago high school had apparently come to terms with such disruptions by pretending they were not occurring. Students kept talking among themselves and blurting out sarcastic comments as he lectured on Italy. "Put your feet on the floor and your elbows on the desk," he finally said to a rambunctious student, almost without breaking verbal stride. "Do you have your book open to the page?" he asked another student, when he was trying to get the class to look at a map of Italy in the textbook. Before many minutes had passed, four students, their eyes closed, had put their heads down on their desks and were oblivious to the teacher, who was now talking about the Pope's reaction to the Reformation. And so it went.

Caught in a milieu in which classmates often disparage conscientiousness about school, many minority students have no countervailing force at home to reinforce the values that the school wishes to instill. Schools in the heart of the city tend to have a sour atmosphere that strips them of the spirit and vitality that might motivate the young. Students, often consumed by poverty, simply do not participate in the kinds of activities that would enrich the school community.

In one urban high school, where the dimly lit corridors and the shabbiness of the building belied its relative newness, there was no cheerleading squad, the band was shrinking from a shortage of members, and the student newspaper had stopped publishing for lack of money. "There is virtually no enthusiasm among the students," said one young woman, an honors student who had found that being chosen editor of the school newspaper was an empty honor. "The kids need incentives to keep them from being down on themselves."

At school and after school, the peer pressure against academic achievement is strong, especially on black males. "The fact that I like to read makes me exceptional at this school," said a young man who was a sophomore at a high school in New Orleans. "Other kids don't want to read, and their parents don't make them study. Some of them seem jealous of me because I go into the school library a lot."

The existence of this negative peer pressure has been documented by such researchers as Signithia Fordham and John Ogbu, who studied a high school in Washington, D.C. They found that fear of being accused of "acting white" created social and psychological pressures against exerting academic effort. "Peer group pressures against academic striving take many forms, including labeling, exclusion from peer activities or ostracism, and physical assault," the researchers said.

Accumulated academic neglect is abundantly evident. In subject after subject, in classroom after classroom, a large portion of the students never encounter subject matter of the sort presented to students of their age in other kinds of schools.

As a result, most graduates of urban high schools serving primarily impoverished minority students have not read and explored the same literature as their counterparts in suburbs and small towns, have not gotten as thorough a grounding in science and mathematics, have not moved into the more sophisticated areas of social studies, have not gained as much proficiency in foreign languages, and have not had as wide an exposure to art and music. The cruel joke is that most of the dropout prevention programs intended to keep them in school set them up to obtain nothing but a meaningless diploma.

The question is, What are urban minority students giving up when they drop out? Michael Sherraden, writing in the *Educational Forum*, said:

In many respects it is inaccurate to view these young people as "dropouts." They never really dropped in. They have attended school, often erratically because school is compulsory and because there are tremendous social pressures to attend. But they had been marginal for many years. They have gone through the motions but they have not been engaged in the educational process. Dropping out is only a visible sign of this underlying pattern of disengagement.

In Cleveland, 11th- and 12th-graders at one high school were taking a course called "Consumer Mathematics" at a point in their education when many of their counterparts in the suburbs were studying calculus. The teacher was leading them through a lesson on the metric system, explaining that it is based on units of 10 and asking them to make calculations of the sort typically assigned in elementary school. They reviewed the problems the teacher had assigned for homework: "8/10 of a kilometer equals how many meters? 3.5 meters equals how many millimeters?"

In a biology class in a New York City high school, students looking at samples of pond water under microscopes were drawing pictures of the rotifers, oligiochaetes, and nematodes they saw. The pictures, however, were as far as they would go, according to the teacher, who said it was his experience that they would not take the next step and learn the distinctions among the organisms.

The possibility of pursuing careers in mathematics and science is foreclosed for most urban minority students long before they finish high school. The result is that, in the entire United States in 1986, of the 3,003 doctorates in the physical sciences awarded to American citizens, only 25 were awarded to blacks and 53 to Hispanics. Of the 1,379 doctorates in engineering awarded to Americans, only 14 were awarded to blacks and 25 to Hispanics.

At a point in the term by which she should have covered 10 chapters in the textbook, a chemistry teacher at a high school in New Orleans had completed just five. "They don't read enough, and only half of them will do the homework assignments," she said. "They tell me my expectations for them are too high, but at this rate they will go off to college at a disadvantage."

This is a high school that sends fewer than 20% of its graduates to college. Those who try to make the leap into higher education are generally at a severe disadvantage because the school offers no physics course, has barely enough students for one calculus class, and offers a maximum of two years of foreign language instruction by a single overworked teacher who must teach every foreign language class in the school. As it is, she said, the students struggle every step of the way in French and Spanish—the only two languages offered—and what they learn in two years is the equivalent of what better-prepared students in suburban high schools learn in one year. "They don't recognize words that are cognates to those in English, because their English vocabulary is so weak," she said.

Data from the American College Testing Program show that, although a large number of minority students say that they plan to enter rigorous programs in higher education, they have generally taken fewer years of college-preparatory courses in English, mathematics, social studies, and natural sciences than non-Hispanic white students.

Some minority students in big cities purposely gravitate toward the lower end of the academic offerings, seeking neither challenge nor substance. "My idea is that it doesn't matter what you're taking just so you can pass it without a problem," said a student at a high school in Houston who was enrolled in a bottom-level mathematics course. "If you move to a higher level and fail, you may as well stay where you were rather than try something you can't accomplish."

Teachers in urban schools are confronted by a dilemma, especially in the upper grades, where the lack of earlier preparation leaves a mark of destruction on young people who are academically ill-prepared. A teacher who asks too much of students who have not been equipped to meet the demands may not only be unrealistic, but may also be setting students up for frustration and failure. On the other hand, not having high expectations for students implies that minority students are incapable of doing the work and dooms them to the ranks of the underclass.

Some students recognize the dilemma. "We should have had a lot more reading and math before we got here," said a 14-year-old in the ninth grade at a Chicago high school, where only 10% of the entering students are able to read at grade level. "The teachers should have been harder on us. We should have been given homework. But I know that if they gave the work, some of the kids wouldn't have done it anyhow."

Homework, in fact, has gone the way of inkwells in the high schools that minority students attend in big cities. Many teachers have simply stopped assigning homework; those who do so have little hope that it will be completed. In a Los Angeles high school located on the edge of Watts, a social studies teacher had set aside part of the class period to let the students start their homework because that was the only homework that most would do. She had put five questions on the board for them to address:

1. Why are natural resources important to a country?
2. What did Thomas Hobbes believe?
3. List some of the reasons for the rise of nations?
4. Explain how England became a nation.
5. What were the causes of the Hundred Years' War?

Twelve of the 26 students listed on the roll were in class. One of the 12 was doing nothing, explaining that he had lost his book. The teacher said that one advantage of letting students do their homework in class was that she could help them. "They can read the words, but sometimes they have comprehension problems," she said. "It is difficult for them to understand concepts. They come to me without a lot of prior knowledge on which to build. I'm lucky if they can identify England as a country."

Given a pool of students in which so many are performing so abysmally, what passes as an honors course at most big-city high schools that serve minority clienteles is a course that draws on the small number of students achieving at or near grade-level. These so-called honors courses usually do not remotely resemble honors courses at good suburban high schools.

In a Cleveland high school that has not offered a College Board Advanced Placement course since 1975, the teacher of an honors English course for seniors said that the best student, the only one who had scored in the top stanine on a standardized reading test, had spent most of the school year in prison. The course was titled Advanced Placement English because it was thought that the designation "might help the students psychologically," even though this was not actually a course that would prepare students for an Advanced Placement exam. Twenty-four students were in the class at the start of the term, but 12 who seldom showed up were dropped. On this day, eight of the remaining 12 were absent.

"I've taught at this school since 1959, when what we called Advanced Placement *was* Advanced Placement," the teacher said. "Now, even in this class, I have to go back and teach about usage and about complex sentences."

She sat quietly for a moment and then spoke of larger problems. "Our students are having children," she said. "Their own mothers are 32 years old, and the house is full of kids. These students can't get the values at home that they need for school. The problems are tremendous, and we don't know how to handle them. These children have given up. I grew up poor and black in the South, but we didn't give up. It's a really sad situation."

Because urban problems have grown so much worse, students in big cities suffer in ways that seem much more resistant to improvement than the educational woes of students elsewhere. Many of the difficulties are not of the school's making and are not within the school's ability to solve, leaving urban education captive to forces beyond its control. Thus impoverished minority students in big cities, who suffer the worst educationally, are doubly afflicted by the ills peculiar to urban life, as well as possible racism.

The network of support systems that surrounds the urban poor is an Ottoman Empire of services, old and creaky, inefficient, and out of touch with changing needs. Life on welfare has become a devastating cycle of indigence, neither adequate to meet a family's needs nor designed to breed self-sufficiency. Structural unemployment has embedded itself in a way that makes a mockery of job training and robs the underclass of the dignity of productive work. Housing for the poor is an embarrassment of paltry contrivances in a land of manicured suburbs and sumptuous condominiums.

Health delivery is inadequate and fragmented, haunting the poor from the moment of conception to the moment of death.

The justice system is an oxymoron, since it provides scant justice and is too disjointed to be a true system. It has been stripped of all pretense of rehabilitation and does little more than put souls on ice, as Eldridge Cleaver once said.

In recent years reports have circulated of reading scores in big-city districts that surpass national norms on standardized tests. But one who visits urban high schools quickly discovers a gap between the reality of the work of most students and the overall scores. The questions raised by Friends of Education about the misleading naure of the above-average scores cut to the heart of the issue. If minority students in urban elementary schools are in fact reaching national norms, then these levels of achievement do not seem to be sustained in the high schools. If minority students are bringing higher scores with them to high school, those higher achievement levels do not appear to be used as a base for serious academic work appropriate to high school.

Part of the difficulty lies in the teaching. For every student inspired by a teacher, too often there is another turned off by a teacher unequipped to deal with the needs of disadvantaged children. The differences among teachers could not have been more vivid than in a Chicago junior high school in which the same group of eighth-graders was taught one period by a teacher for whom the students were well-behaved and responsive and the next period by a teacher whose rapport with them was so poor that they were disruptive and uninvolved.

In New Orleans a teacher in an American history course was presenting a unit on black Americans in connection with Black History Week. One by one he recited the names: Gwendolyn Brooks, Ralph Bunche, George Washington Carver, Frederick Douglas, rattling off a long list of dates and facts about each. No questions, no discussion, no interpretation. The students spent the entire period with their heads down, copying facts as the teacher dictated them—information that might better have been presented in a handout or assigned to the students to look up on their own.

Yet another teacher, this one at an elementary school in Houston, was confusing fourth-graders one day with an elaborate reading lesson on "eye syllables that we see" and "ear syllables that we hear." The students were identifying the two kinds of syllables as they went through a story instead of reading for enjoyment and comprehension.

Urban schools have no monopoly on uninspired teaching, but it takes a terrible toll on students who are already unmotivated. Students from advantaged backgrounds will often persevere despite poor teaching because of the rewards they expect by staying the course and earning their credentials. Delayed gratification seldom is enough to hold those who have no experience of reaping rewards that have been held in abeyance. The lack of success of minority students in urban schools is so prevalent that the expectation of failure is as much a part of many classrooms as the textbooks that the children struggle to read. Remediation is a permanent state of being rather than a temporary intervention.

So widespread are low expectations that, when a student in Los Angeles wanted to take algebra, she was dissuaded by a teacher who warned that it was too difficult for her and steered her into an easier course. Last spring, three years later, that same student, still steadfast in the face of discouragement, had shaken free of the ill-founded advice and was taking Advanced Placement calculus.

High schools in the inner city must become more like elementary schools, proffering supportive environments that bolster the confidence of students. Experts repeatedly reaffirm the merits of smallness, and yet urban high schools remain Goliaths, as though there were virtue in bigness. Urban high schools must insinuate themselves into the lives of students in ways that make the schools places where students want to be. The schools should present themselves to students not as places where they can work toward a better "tomorrow," but as places where they can create a better "today."

Building a sense of community among students can put the school in a position to foster the values essential for academic success. Students should help set the rules of the community and participate in its upkeep, as they do in Japanese schools and in some American boarding schools. There should be activities involving groups of students and teachers, so that bonding is enhanced and students feel that they belong to the school and the school belongs to them.

A high school of 200 to 300 students with a faculty of its own that is shared with no other school—even though schools may co-exist on separate floors in the same building—can be an intimate institution in which students see the same small cadre of teachers

over and over again. Time must be built into the schedule for
teachers to meet regularly for several hours a week with small
groups of students to talk about life and its problems. More effort
must be made to inform the adults at home about what students
are studying, so that the adults will take more interest in what is
occurring in the classroom.

Borrowing from Theodore Sizer's Coalition of Essential
Schools, urban high schools must embrace the philosophy that
"less is more." The scope of the curriculum should be reduced
and focused on a more limited body of material that can be taught
in depth—adapted to individual needs along the way—so that it
is better understood and serves as a possible base for widening interests.

Improving the big-city high schools that are attended largely
by black and Hispanic students is possible. A pitifully few scat-
tered instances have demonstrated that with fundamental restructuring it can be done. But there is a tendency to revel in
delusions of improvement. Order may be restored, but oppression reigns. Test scores may rise, but concepts remain ungrasped.
Facts may be memorized, but students cannot apply them in solving problems. Dropouts may be kept in school, but the diplomas
they receive are not backed by skills and knowledge.

Nonetheless, some students persist, hoping that school can
lead to a life better than the one they have known. A student in
Houston, who said that his parents showed little interest in his education, found his reinforcement in a letter written to him by his
older sister. He pulled it from his back pocket, where he said he
always carried it, and unfolded the creased, dog-eared stationery.
His sister had set out a philosophy that she summed up in just a
few words: "Love, Goals, Education, Drive, Resourcefulness, Perseverance, God."

THE NEW UNTOUCHABLES[2]

On an average morning in Chicago, about 5,700 children in 190 classrooms come to school only to find they have no teacher. Victimized by endemic funding shortages, the system can't afford sufficient substitutes to take the place of missing teachers. "We've been in this typing class a whole semester," says a 15-year-old at Du Sable High, "and they still can't find us a teacher."

In a class of 39 children at Chicago's Goudy Elementary School, an adult is screaming at a child: "Keisha, look at me . . . Look me in in the eye!" Keisha is fighting with a classmate. Over what? It turns out: over a crayon, said The Chicago Tribune in 1988. Last January the underfunded school began rationing supplies.

The odds these black kids in Chicago face are only slightly worse than those faced by low-income children all over America. Children like these will be the parents of the year 2000. Many of them will be unable to earn a living and fulfill the obligations of adults; they will see their families disintegrate, their children lost to drugs and destitution. When we later condemn them for "parental failings," as we inevitably will do, we may be forced to stop and remember how we also failed them in the first years of their lives.

It is a commonplace that a society reveals its reverence or contempt for history by the respect or disregard that it displays for older people. The way we treat our children tells us something of the future we envision. The willingness of the nation to relegate so many of these poorly housed and poorly fed and poorly educated children to the role of outcasts in a rich society is going to come back to haunt us.

With nearly 30 percent of high-school students dropping out before they graduate—60 percent in segregated high schools—it is not surprising that illiteracy figures have continued to grow worse. The much publicized volunteer literary movement promoted for the last six years by Barbara Bush serves only 200,000

[2]Reprint of an article by Jonathan Kozol, author and commentator on education. From NEWSWEEK, Winter 1989/Spring 1990 © 1990, Newsweek, Inc. All rights reserved. Reprinted by permission.

of the nation's estimated 30 million functional illiterates. Meanwhile, the gulf in income between rich and poor American families is wider than at any time since figures we recorded, starting in the 1940s. The richest 20 percent received 44 percent of national family income; the poorest 20 percent got only 4.6 percent. More than 5 million of the poorest group are children.

Disparities in wealth play out in financing of schools. Low-income children, who receive the least at home, receive the least from public education. New Trier High School, for example, serving children from such affluent suburbs as Winnetka, Ill., pays its better teachers 50 percent above the highest paid teachers at Du Sable, by no means the worst school in Chicago. The public schools in affluent Great Neck and White Plains, N.Y., spend twice as much per pupil as the schools that serve the children of the Bronx.

Infant-mortality figures, classic indices of health in most societies, have also worsened for poor children and especially for nonwhite children. The gap between white and black mortality in children continues to widen, reaching a 47-year high in 1987 (the most recent year for which data are available.) Black children are more than twice as likely to die in infancy as whites—nine times as likely to be neurologically impaired. One possible consequence: black children are three times as likely as whites to be identified as mentally retarded by their public schools.

Federal programs initiated in the 1960s to assist low-income children, though far from universally successful, made solid gains in preschool education (Head Start), compensatory reading (Chapter I) and precollege preparation (Upward Bound), while sharply cutting the rates of infant death and child malnutrition. Limited funding, however, narrowed the scope of all these efforts. Head Start, for example, never has reached more than one of five low-income children between its start-up in the '60s and today.

Rather than expand these programs, President Reagan kept them frozen or else cut them to the bone. Living stipends paid to welfare families with children dropped to 35 percent (adjusted for inflation) below the 1970 level. Nearly half a million families lost all welfare payments. A million people were cut from food stamps. Two million kids were dropped from school-lunch programs. The WIC program (Women, Infants, Children), which provides emergency nutrition supplements to low-income infants, young children and pregnant women, was another target of Reagan administration cuts, but Congress successfully fought them off. Despite their efforts, the WIC budget is woefully inadequate, and has never been able to provide services to even half of the children and women who meet the eligibility requirements.

Federal housing funds were also slashed during these years. As these cutbacks took their tolls, homeless children were seen begging in the streets of major cities for the first time since the Great Depression. A fivefold increase in homeless children was seen in Washington, D.C., in 1986 alone. By 1987 nearly half the occupants of homeless shelters in New York City were children. The average homeless child was only 6 years old.

The lives of homeless children tell us much of the disregard that society has shown for vulnerable people. Many of these kids grow up surrounded by infectious illnesses no longer seen in most developed nations. Whooping cough and tuberculosis, once regarded as archaic illnesses, are now familiar in the shelters. Shocking numbers of these children have not been inoculated and for this reason cannot go to school. Those who do are likely to be two years behind grade level.

Many get to class so tired and hungry that they cannot concentrate. Others are ashamed to go to school because of shunning by their peers. Classmates label them "the hotel children" and don't want to sit beside them. Even their teachers sometimes keep their distance. The children look diseased and dirty. Many times they are. Often unable to bathe, they bring the smell of destitution with them into school. There *is* a smell of destitution, I may add. It is the smell of sweat and filth and urine. Like many journalists, I often find myself ashamed to be resisting the affection of a tiny child whose entire being seems to emanate pathology.

So, in a terrifying sense, these children have become American untouchables. Far from demonstrating more compassion, administration leaders have resorted to a stylized severity in speaking of poor children. Children denied the opportunity for Head Start, sometimes health care, housing, even certified schoolteachers, have nonetheless been told by William J. Bennett, preaching from his bully pulpit as U.S. secretary of Education under Reagan, that they would be held henceforth to "higher standards." Their parents—themselves too frequently the products of dysfunctional and underfunded urban schools—have nonetheless been lectured on their "lack of values." Efforts begun more than 10 years ago to equalize school funding between districts have been put on the back burner and are now replaced by strident exhortations to the poor to summon "higher motivation" and, no matter how debilitated by disease or hunger, to "stand tall." Celebrities are hired to sell children on the wisdom of not dropping out of school. The White House tells them they should "just say no" to the temptations of the streets. But hope cannot be marketed as easily as blue jeans. Certain realities—race and class and caste—are there and they remain.

What is the consequence of tougher rhetoric and more severe demands? Higher standards, in the absence of authentic educative opportunities in early years, function as a punitive attack on those who have been cheated since their infancy. Effectively, we now ask more of those to whom we now give less. Earlier testing for schoolchildren is prescribed. Those who fail are penalized by being held back from promotion and by being slotted into lower tracks where they cannot impede the progress of more privileged children. Those who disrupt classroom discipline are not placed in smaller classes with more patient teachers; instead, at a certain point, they are expelled—even if this means expulsion of a quarter of all pupils in the school. The pedagogic hero of the Reagan White House was Joe Clark—a principal who roamed the hallways of his segregated high school in New Jersey with a bullhorn and a bat and managed to raise reading scores by throwing out his low-achieving pupils.

In order to justify its abdication, the federal government has called for private business to assist the underfunded urban schools. While business leaders have responded with some money, they have also brought a very special set of values and priorities. The primary concern of business is the future productivity of citizens. Education is regarded as capital investment. The child is seen as raw material that needs a certain processing before it is of value. The question posed, therefore, is how much money it is worth investing in a certain child to obtain a certain economic gain. Educators, eager to win corporate support, tell business leaders what they want to hear. "We must start thinking of students as workers," says the head of the American Federation of Teachers, Albert Shanker.

The notion of kids as workers raises an unprecedented question. Is future productivity the only rationale for their existence?

A lot of the things that make existence wonderful are locked out of the lives of children seen primarily as future clerical assistants or as possible recruits to office pools at IBM. The other consequence of "productivity" thinking is an increased willingness to make predictions about children, based almost entirely on their social status. Those whose present station seems to promise most are given most. Those whose origins are least auspicious are provided with stripped-down education. IQ testing of low-income babies has been recently proposed in order to identify those who are particularly intelligent and to accord them greater educational advantages, although this means that other babies will be stigmatized by their exclusion.

A heightened discrimination in the use of language points to a dual vision: we speak of the need to "train" the poor, but "educate" the children of the middle class and rich. References to "different learning styles" and the need to "target" different children with "appropriate" curricula are now becoming fashionable ways of justifying stratified approaches. Early tracking is one grim result. A virtual retreat from any efforts at desegregation is another: if children of different social classes need "appropriate" and "different" offerings, it is more efficient and sensible to teach them separately.

A century ago, Lord Acton spoke thus of the United States: "In a country where there is no distinction of class a child is not born to the station of its parents, but with an indefinite claim to all the prizes that can be won by thought and labor. It is in conformity with the theory of equality . . . to give as near as possible to every youth an equal start in life." Americans, he said, "are unwilling that any should be deprived in childhood of the means of competition."

That this tradition has been utterly betrayed in recent years is now self-evident. The sense of fairness, however, runs deep in the thinking of Americans. Though frequently eclipsed, it is a theme that stubbornly recurs. A quarter century ago, it took disruptions in the streets to force Americans to question the unfairness of de jure segregation. Today it is not law but economics that condemns the children of the very poor to the implacable inheritance of a diminished destiny. "No matter what they do," says the superintendent of Chicago's public schools, "their lot has been determined."

Between the dream and the reality there falls the shadow of the ghetto school, the ghetto hospital, the homeless shelter. Appeals to the pocketbook have done no good. Black leaders have begun to contemplate the need for massive protests by poor people. Middle-class students, viscerally shocked by the hard edge of poverty they see in city streets, may be disposed to join them. The price may be another decade of societal disruption. The reward may be the possibility that we can enter the next century not as two nations, vividly unequal, but as the truly democratic nation we profess to be and have the power to become. Whether enough people think this outcome worth the price, however, is by no means clear.

A SCHOOL SYSTEM NEAR MELTDOWN[3]

To begin to understand the problems of the Chicago public schools, consider the state law that gives any teacher charged with incompetence an entire year to shape up while continuing in the classroom. Some principals say the dismissal procedures are so complicated, they don't even try; some "bad apples" are simply transferred from school to school. In a devastating seven-month investigation of the school system, the Chicago Tribune examined the case of Grace Currin, who has taught in four different schools in the last five years. This year her principal at Spencer Elementary School reportedly determined that every one of her 22 fourth graders needs to attend summer school because Currin did not prepare them for fifth grade.

On any given day, 45,000 Chicago public-school students—one in nine—are absent. But many are just following their teacher's lead. In May some 1,250 teachers—5 percent of the total—called in sick each day. The Board of Education does not have enough substitutes, so as many as 11,160 students were teacherless. In one unattended class at Austin High, students recently poured water on the desks and ripped down a bulletin board.

[3]Reprint of an article by Melinda Beck of *Newsweek*. From NEWSWEEK, 112: 60–1. Jl 4 '88. Copyright © 1988 by Newsweek, Inc. All rights reserved. Reprinted with permission.

"You can tell the view an institution holds by its washrooms," says George Schmidt, leader of a dissident teachers-union faction. Toilet paper is chronically in short supply. At Orr, a west-side high school, janitors don't restock it because kids just ball up the paper with water and throw it at the ceiling, explains one teacher, who keeps tissue in her classroom for her students to use. Sadly, some kids don't have toilet paper at home, either. According to one report, a Goudy Elementary teacher visiting a home was appalled to find the family using pages of school library books instead.

There are dismal conditions in urban schools all across America. But in Chicago the entire system seems riddled with decay. Education Secretary William Bennett has repeatedly called it the "worst" in the nation. "You have close to an educational meltdown," he said last fall. The ingredients include a bloated bureaucracy, a powerful teachers union that has struck nine times in 19 years and some of the worst demographic and social problems in the country. The result: roughly half of Chicago's public-school students drop out before graduation. Of those who remain, only one-third can read at or above the national average. When American College Test scores were averaged, half the city's high schools ranked in the lowest 1 percent nationally.

This week the Illinois Legislature is scrambling to consider a host of school-reform proposals, including a 40 percent state-tax increase Gov. James Thompson wants to devote largely to education. But cynics say the measures will not even begin to address the system's deeper woes. The Chicago Tribune series last month charged school administrators with "institutionalized child neglect" and concluded in an editorial that the only remedy is a voucher system that would let parents send their kids to private schools instead.

Chicago education officials angrily deny that conditions are that terrible, and tend to blame each other for the problems. "We were the first board to stand up to the union," boasts Board of Education president Frank Gardner, though the 4 percent wage increase it agreed to in a 19-day teachers' strike last fall will contribute to a projected $188 million deficit. "We are not obstructionist. We are promoting educational reforms," says Chicago Teachers Union president Jacqueline Vaughn, who blames school administrators for "feathering their nests" while some teachers spend their own money for supplies. "Your real problem is underfunding," says school superintendent Manford Byrd, who earns $100,000 a year and contends that the recent $22 million reconstruction of the plush central office was not excessive, even though some schools lack basic facilities such as gyms and faculty copy machines. "If the system is educationally bankrupt, it just didn't happen," Byrd adds. "[Reform] should have been done 10 or 12 years ago."

Indeed, the seeds of Chicago's school collapse were sown long ago in the city's deep racial and ethnic divisions and its ingrown political power structure. In the 1960s Richard Daley, who was then mayor, typically bought educational peace by acceding to CTU demands. When money grew tight, the Board of Education gave the union power instead; now even curriculum changes and blackboard space are part of contract talks. Meanwhile, the central-school bureaucracy has burgeoned. Of its 42, 167 employees, only slightly more than half are teachers. ("All of the rewards are geared toward getting [teachers] out of the classroom and into the money," says Schmidt.) Since 1971, the overall budget has swelled from $719 million to $1.9 billion, while the student population has shrunk 27 percent.

Much of that loss came from "white flight"—spurred on by a 1980 desegregation plan that backfired. Once half white, the student population is now 87 percent minority, and much of that is hard-core underclass. Some 69 percent of students live at the poverty level. Drug use and discipline problems are endemic, making learning difficult for even the most motivated. Against fire regulations, some principals chain school doors to keep gangs out and students in. Still, Orr teacher Andrea Stewart says some students drop out because they are afraid for their safety.

Under the circumstances, many Chicago educators say they are doing the best they can. "We can't expect our kids to read a lot when they parents don't read a lot," says Leroy Lovelace, an English teacher at all-black Wendell Phillips High. Critics insist that blaming society is a cop-out. "Why are there some public schools that work and some private schools with poor kids that work? It's the stucture of the system," says Michael Bakalis, former state superintendent of education and dean of Loyola University's education school.

Chicago's Roman Catholic schools manage to effectively educate more than 160,000 students with only 32 central-office administrators; in a random sample, every one of 3,000 seventh graders scored above national averages on a standardized test. But public administrators argue that parochial schools, by definition, have motivated parents and enjoy the luxury of turning problem students away. Parental disinterest is part of the problem in the public schools. Parents are now required to pick up their children's report cards twice a year—but many don't show up, so some students never learn their grades.

More Authority: There is no shortage of reform ideas. Most plans would cut the central bureaucracy. Many would also reduce the grace period for incompetent teachers to around 45 days and give principals more authority over teachers. (Union chief Vaughn resists that idea. "How does hiring and firing ensure student achievement?" she asks, sidestepping the notion that it might encourage achievement by *teachers*.) The union has offered to waive some contract provisions in favor of "school-based management" plans that would give teachers, principals and parents more autonomy in running individual schools.

Bennett, for his part, endorsed the Tribune's voucher idea. "You've got to take power away from some who have it and give it to the consumers," he told a Chicago group this month. But critics argue that such a plan could destroy the public schools, dramatically increase costs and penalize students whose parents are not interested enough to "shop" for better schools.

No voucher plan is likely to be accepted soon. Late last week state lawmakers were stalemated over a plan to create 20 separate school districts in Chicago, which might serve to add still more bureaucracy.

And if the legislature doesn't approve the governor's proposed tax hike, the Board of Education will be forced to "further cannibalize the school system," warns board spokesman Bob Saigh. Clearly, money alone will not solve the problems; at $4,373 per pupil, Chicago already spends more than the national average. "Everyone has to work to improve the schools—parents, business communicators, educators, ministers," says Louella Williams, an Orr parent who has volunteered in the system for 20 years. Chicago's public schools desperately need more parents like her, and more teachers, administrators and politicians who are willing to put the interests of pupils above their own. If not, students may take away only one grim lesson: that no one cared enough to give them a future.

THE ILLINOIS EXPERIENCE[4]

In the summer of 1987 the Illinois State Board of Education established a major program objective for 1987 through 1991: that the board "adopt, strengthen, and expand policies, procedures, and programs which address the problems of at-risk children and youth." Six areas of emphasis were identified under this objective: early intervention, early childhood education, minority achievement, urban education, truancy prevention, and alternative education.

In order to address these areas in new ways, the board simultaneously created the Urban Education Partnership Grants program. Because the needs of today's students have become so complex that they are outstripping the services of the agencies and schools that were created to serve them, collaborative partnerships must be established that involve schools, families, businesses, social service agencies, and other groups in an effort to coordinate resources, solve problems, and provide more chances for student success. Urban Partnership Grants are designed to enable schools with high concentrations of at-risk students to develop and implement new strategies to meet the multifaceted needs of these youngsters.

Money from Chapter 2 of the Education Consolidation and Improvement Act of 1981 is used to fund the grants. A unique feature of these grants is that they are school-based and require the participation of the principal, the school staff, the parents, and a variety of partners from the community.

RATIONALE

For more than three decades, we have assigned schools a myriad of tasks—including, but not limited to, developing students' academic achievement, helping individuals contribute to and flourish in society, enhancing social equality and social progress, and increasing understanding of cultural diversity. Historically,

[4]Reprint of an article by Warren Chapman, an educational consultant for the Illinois State Board of Education. Reprinted by permission from *Phi Delta Kappan*, Ja '91 72: 355-8. Copyright © 1991 by *Phi Delta Kappa*. Reprinted with permission of author.

schools have been granted a great deal of autonomy in carrying out these tasks. Society did not challenge the schools as long as it seemed that the assigned tasks were being accomplished satisfactorily. For decades schools have succeeded or failed with only minimal input and assistance from the families, communities, and businesses they serve.

Today, however, the tasks assigned to schools and the public's expectations for them have changed dramatically. In addition to the earlier requirements, we now ask schools to Americanize immigrants, to delay the entry of young people into the labor market, to serve as custodians of children during certain hours of the day, to help desegregate society, to battle drug abuse, to improve the health of students, and to solve a variety of other social problems.

Though we have expanded the responsibility of the public schools to provide social services to students and their families, we have failed to supply additional resources to fund these new services. Several national groups have recognized the complexity of the problems facing today's schools and have acknowledged that the resources of the schools alone are insufficient to deal with them. Recent statements from the Council of the Great City Schools, the Council of Chief State School Officers, and the Education Commission of the States have called the coordination of children's services, especially in urban areas, a top national priority. These groups are encouraging schools in urban areas to forge more effective connections with social service agencies, community-based organizations, and businesses.

The development of these links will take a great deal of effort, because both the schools and the social service agencies are accustomed to operating autonomously. To date, connections between schools, families, and other community groups have been few in number and inconsistent in quality.

URBAN EDUCATION AND PARTNERSHIPS

The Illinois school reform program of 1985 established goals and strategies designed to improve educational outcomes. One major goal was to improve the education of students who reside in the state's urban communities. Although all schools needed to work to improve their programs and increase their students' chances for success, it was clear that education reform in urban school districts had to take different forms because of the size, complexity, demography, and other characteristics of urban centers. While the problems that face urban schools are severe and the issues complex, innovation and hard work can go a long way toward solving the problems and resolving the issues.

During the 1987–88 school year the state board in Illinois began to foster urban school reform by awarding grants demonstration programs through the Urban Education Partnership Grants program. Three major principles guide the program.

• Problems facing urban schools can be solved through collaboration and partnership between the schools and business, government, social service agencies, and community groups. Therefore, efforts should be made to improve the communication and cooperation of schools with other government offices and agencies, including those dealing with housing, health, and welfare at the state, county, and municipal levels. Schools should also be encouraged to communicate and cooperate with parents and with institutions in the private sector that are concerned with a well-educated citizenry.

• The objectives, programs, and practices supported by the grants must enhance educational equity. This principle established a firm commitment to integration, recognizes the pluralism of society and of the student body, and encourages diversity, options, and choices. It is intended to help restore public confidence in the schools' ability to provide educational services to a diverse student population through programs that respond to the cultures of the students served.

• Nationwide networking with other agencies and institutions is essential for information sharing, data collection, and resource development. Programs and practices that have beem successful in a single urban school district should be recognized and shared with other districts. The grant program also encourages continuous evaluation of programs and practices and the reporting of findings to the public.

During the past three years, more than 30 two-year projects were funded by the Urban Education Partnership Grants program. The grants (ranging in value to a maximum of $30,000 per year) were awarded directly to schools, not to districts, and all were designed to support programs and activities that focus on improving student outcomes. The principals, as the project directors, identified the needs in their schools and, with input from parents and teachers, proposed programs to address those needs at the school level.

The projects were to be evaluated by objective measures of outcomes, including (but not limited to) improved student attendance, higher standardized test scores, improved grades, increased parent involvement, and decreased discipline problems. Each school that applied for a grant proposed a design for an educational program to improve outcomes through a collaborative effort or partnership involving at least one parent or community group, social service agency, government agency, or business. The grants were awarded to schools according to how well the applicants explained their partnerships and how well the proposed partnerships addressed the pressing intellectual and social needs of youngsters at risk of failing. Members of the staff of the state board of education provided technical assistance.

PARTNERSHIPS AND PARENT INVOLVEMENT

Partnerships promote links between institutions that make each stronger than it is on its own. But partnerships also give the community new insights into the problems and successes of educators and provide opportunities for parents and other citizens to make meaningful contributions to the schools. Many partnerships promote home/school interaction and enable principals and teachers to make better use of external resources.

The work of Joyce Epstein was seminal in establishing parent involvement guidelines for the Urban Education Partnership Grants program. Epstein has documented how important it is for state departments to foster meaningful parent involvement programs in schools by providing both financial and technical support.

School districts and school administrators are strongly influenced by state policies, guidelines, and funding for educational programs. Through their policies and actions, state agencies either recognize or ignore the connections between the educational and socializing institutions in children's lives, particularly families and schools. Illinois wanted to emphasize that the quality of family/school connections can dramatically affect the academic and social development of children.

Staff members with the Illinois program encouraged all schools applying for grants to take into account the five elements of Epstein's model of parent involvement:

• basic obligations of families, including health, safety, and a positive home environment;

• basic obligations of schools, including communication with parents regarding their child's programs and progress;

• parent involvement at school, including volunteer activities and support for sports, student performances, and other activities;

• parent involvement in learning activities at home, including supervising homework and helping children work on skills that will help them learn in the classroom; and

• parent involvement in governance, decision making, and advocacy, including participation in parent/teacher organizations and in various decision-making and advisory roles.

A majority of the programs that have been funded by the Illinois Urban Education Partnership Grants program have included one or more types of parent involvement, as illustrated in the examples described below.

Project A. School A is an inner-city elementary school. Most of its students are Hispanic, and most have limited skills in speaking and writing English. Historically, students at School A scored below grade level on written and verbal sections of the district's standardized tests. Parent involvement at the school had been limited, mainly because the school was unable to involve parents creatively in meaningful activities.

The school applied for and was awarded an Urban Partnership Grant. The main focus of its proposal was to improve the language and writing skills of students in the primary grades through a whole-language approach.

The grant include support for students to go on field trips to museums, to the zoo, and to other educational events. A group of parents accompanied the students and teachers on these trips. After the trips, the students returned to the school and told stories of their experiences to the parents, who encouraged children to give as much detail as possible and who acted as scribes, writing down what the children said in Spanish or in English. Parents who were not able to participate in the field trips were encouraged to write down stories for their own children at home. Each child's dictated work was collected throughout the year in a portfolio.

By the end of the school year, one could see that in virtually every instance students were telling stories of their experiences in greater detail, using larger vocabularies, and creating sentences that were more complex than had been the case at the beginning of the school year. In addition, parents who were involved in this program improved their own vocabularies and writing skills. Most important, parents learned how to assist their own children in learning at home. Teachers and parents learned how to work together in ways that improved the academic achievement of students.

Project B. School B is a suburban junior high school with a racially diverse student body. For several years, test scores of students at the school had been declining. Only about 40% of the students turned in assigned homework. Although parents were concerned about the education of their children, the school conducted few activities that allowed parents to help with their children's education.

The project funded by the school's Urban Partnership Grant focused on raising students' test scores and improving their report card grades. The project had three main components. First, it established a homework lab that was available to students two days a week. Three classroom teachers were on hand to give assistance when needed, and students learned to help one another with assignments. Targeted students were assigned to the lab by their teachers, but many other students chose to attend the lab to do their homework, rather than to go home to an empty house. As time passed, the homework lab became more and more popular. Soon it was the "in" place to be—and not just for students. Teachers also started to stay after school when it became clear that the students wanted individualized help.

The second component of School B's project was the establishment of "improvement contracts" for individual students. Each participating student met with a counselor to draw up a contract setting the goal of raising report card grades in three subject areas. The contract was then signed by the student, the teacher or teachers involved, and the student's parent(s). These contracts proved very influential in establishing meaningful communication between teachers and parents. The structure they established gave parents a reason to monitor both homework and schoolwork regularly. Parents, teachers, and students received immediate feedback about the students' academic progress.

The third phase of the project was the most distinctive. Since 90% of School B's students had VCRs in their homes, the school produced instructional videotapes in cooperation with the local cable company. This joint venture resulted in two series of tapes: a video bank of "critical lessons" and a parent education series.

The parent education tapes showed parents effective ways to motivate their children to learn. For example, one tape concentrated on teaching parents to observe their children's study habits and organizational skills. The tape then provided ways to motivate children to improve—other than by yelling, threats, or bribery.

The critical lessons were taped class sessions that students could use as instructional supplements. These videos covered a number of topics in mathematics, English, and social studies, including the U.S. Constitution and how to write a research paper. Each tape allowed students and their parents to view a class and to study the important points of the lesson. This enabled parents to discuss substantive ideas with their children and to become actively involved in their children's learning. This innovative use of new technology acknowledged the fact that many parents cannot come to school to see what their children are learning. Thus the project did the next best thing: it brought the school to the parents.

The Urban Education Partnership Grants program also funded projects at other schools that fostered and documented parent involvement of various kinds. For example, throughout the year at one school, a "welcome wagon" gave parents new to the school information about the school, about their children's grade levels, and about ways to become involved in their children's education. Home visits by the principal and other staff members and parent-to-parent exchanges also brought information about the school directly into parents' homes.

Some funded projects helped to improve school newsletters; others provided translators for parents who did not understand English well. Still other projects made use of the telephone as a way of communicating with parents. One school used trained parent volunteers in a home-work center, and several schools organized parent volunteers to work in classrooms with at-risk students or with those lacking proficiency in English. Parent volunteers in some schools served as translators at meetings of the parent/teacher organization.

WHAT HAVE WE LEARNED?

The Illinois experience with the awarding of sizable, multi-year, competitive grants may prove helpful to others states. Through the use of grant-funded demonstration projects that design, implement, and evaluate combined approaches to school improvement and parent involvement, we have learned valuable lessons about altering the practices of the participating schools and those of other schools that benefit from the experience at the demonstration sites.

First, we learned that multi-year grants are important. Most state grants are awarded for a single year, but it often takes longer than a year to see progress in improving urban schools and involving parents. With support that lasts longer, the schools are able to establish and stabilize their programs.

We also learned that it is important to consider multiple outcomes, not just scores on achievement tests. Improving scores on achievement tests takes longer than improving other measures of school success, such as attendance, discipline, report card grades, level of parent involvement, and so on.

The funded programs were highly successful. The grants energized the schools that received them and helped increase parent involvement over the course of the grant periods. Outside evaluators hired by the Illinois State Board of Education to determine whether the schools were meeting their stated goals confirmed that parent involvement affected student achievement and that many more parents had become involved with their children's education as a result of the schools' efforts. The evaluators interviewed people in 20 of the schools that received grants and collected quantitative and qualitative data that showed that 87% of the schools in the program accomplished more than 90% of their stated goals. This evidence that such low-cost strategies yield relatively high returns is very encouraging.

A BLUEPRINT FOR BETTER SCHOOLS[5]

Dante Hooker is only 10 years old, still too young to know the odds are against him.

From his back-row desk in Barbara Neilander's fourth-grade classroom at Martin Luther King Elementary School in Rochester, N.Y., he tries hard to keep up with 5 hours a day of reading, writing and arithmetic. So far, he's succeeding. But his teacher worries that, as he gets older, his motivation will fade, and so will his chances of attending college or getting a good job. "I tell him to keep going," says his mother, Nettie Lloyd, who has raised Dante and five older children. "I hope he'll be different"—different from his father and two of his brothers, none of whom made it past the ninth grade. But when she sends him off each morning from their home in the Harriet Tubman Estates housing project, she knows that if he is to make it, he will need a lot of help, the kind of help she can't provide.

Fortunately, Dante Hooker may get that help. The Rochester school district is striving to change the odds for him and many of the 33,000 other students in the city's public schools. A new contract that makes Rochester's teachers among the highest paid anywhere—with some salaries to hit $70,000—is the most visible sign of that effort. The contract is only one element of a community-wide initiative that could radically alter how the city's schools are run and become a model of reform for 15,000 school districts across America.

Rochester's blueprint for change is based largely on *A Nation Prepared: Teachers for the 21st Century*, a 1986 report by the Carnegie Forum on Education and the Economy that proposed an overhaul of how teachers teach and what students learn. The experts behind the report recognized that any national reform effort would flop unless local educators first came up with plans of their own. Rochester, taking up the challenge, last week released its response, entitled *A Region Prepared*.

[5]Reprint of an article by Jerry Buckley for *U.S. News & World Report*. Copyright, January 18, 1989, U.S. News & World Report.

Ready for the workplace

It's an ambitious plan that will shift much of the decision making to teachers and administrators in individual schools and make them more accountable for student performance. It calls for changes in the training and hiring of teachers, with an emphasis on minority recruitment. And it goes beyond the Carnegie report to target "at risk" students, which for Rochester is the bulk of the school population. The city aims to turn out students who can read, write, compute, use technology and be ready for the workplace. Even more, it wants to produce students with discipline, self-determination and self-respect.

But community leaders know that talking about improving schools is one thing; doing it is another. The contract that preceded last week's report is a high-stakes gamble, a $31 million venture that critics fear will prove too expensive and do little to upgrade student achievement. "We bought a concept but not all that many specifics," says school-board member Archie Curry, who voted against the pact. "I'm worried that it will end up being business as usual, except that the teachers are getting paid more money."

Much has yet to be worked out, it is true, but national education experts say Rochester's experiment is further along than any in America. If it works, these experts say, cities across the country may follow suit. "If Rochester can do it, it can be done most anywhere," says Arkansas Governor Bill Clinton, who notes that Rochester's effort started from within and is directed at the grass-roots level. "It gives the rest of us hope."

Education will be mentioned often in this year's presidential race. And it's a major concern of a well-known noncandidate, New York Governor Mario Cuomo, who last week announced the formation in Rochester of the National Center on Education and the Economy. New York's initial $1 million contribution likely will lead to more money from national foundations and local sources. Eleven educational and business institutions in the area formed the Rochester Education Council, which will work with the national center to help implement the lofty ideals of the teachers contract. Heading both the center and the local council will be Marc Tucker, formerly the Carnegie Forum's executive director. Rochester is an ideal education laboratory, says Cuomo. "What we need are good ideas and practical applications. Rochester is a chance to think, analyze and apply the answers to real-life problems."

That Rochester has even reached this point—and has a fair chance of succeeding—is due to an unusual coalition of individuals for whom Rochester is an adopted home. They include the Boston-born superintendent of schools, a Polish immigrant who directs the teachers union, the Mormon head of Eastman Kodak, a Chicago native who is president of the University of Rochester and a black Virginian who leads the Urban League of Rochester. The project's modest start and its hope for real progress also reflect the Main Street character of a city where craftsmen and blue-collar workers have long combined with professors and scientists to create diversity and a sense of community. "This city deep down believes it can solve its problems," says Dennis O'Brien, U. of R.'s president. "We're all different, but there's a belief that if we yell at each other long enough, somehow we'll get it right."

Philharmonic and poverty

To most outsiders, Rochester is just a cold spot on the shore of Lake Ontario. The city of 236,000, surrounded by 464,000 suburbanites, is rarely mentioned as an example of urban woes. But visitors soon learn that it's not a lily-white community whose most pressing concern is snow removal. The city has its philharmonic but also its poverty. Affordable housing, adequate health care and good jobs are in short supply for many city residents. For teenagers, pregnancies, alcohol, drugs and dropouts are all part of the same sad résumé. In Rochester, as elsewhere, one place people look for answers—the school system—is part of the problem.

Most of the descendants of the Irish, Italian and German immigrants who helped build Rochester have moved to the suburbs, to towns with names like Pittsford, Penfield and Brighton. They send their children to top-rank public and parochial schools where teachers sometimes worry about students who work *too hard*. Rochester's East Avenue, with its stone churches and gracious mansions, remains a grand boulevard, and many nearby middle-class neighborhoods, lined with big clapboard houses, have been rejuvenated in recent years. But after business hours, many downtown streets are deserted and crime is common in several sections. For most suburbanites, "downtown" is a faraway place to be avoided except for a trip to a museum or a hocky game at the War Memorial.

Many who stay in the city are poor whites, blacks and Hispanics and, more recently, refugees from Asia. Their children are the city school system's main clients. They go to schools with names quintessentially American: Benjamin Franklin, Theodore Roosevelt, Thomas Edison, Frederick Douglass. Half of Rochester's 47 schools are over 60 years old. What they produce is also quintessentially American.

No place for dropouts

The nation's demographic destiny—an increasingly non-white, badly educated, low-skilled work force—is clearly evident in Rochester. As the home of Kodak, Xerox and Bausch & Lomb, the city has boasted a high share of high-tech jobs. But over the past two decades, just as the workplace became more complex and demanding and foreign competition intensified, the basic skills of students coming from Rochester's public schools slumped sharply. The days when a teenager could quit school and start a long career at Kodak are long gone. The assembly line is still there, but it's different. No one knows that better than Kay Whitmore, Kodak's president. With 45,000 employees in the area, Kodak dominates Rochester's economy. "Kodak's future depends on its work force," Whitmore says. "Five years from now, even if we get all the qualified job seekers from the Rochester suburbs, we still won't have enough. If we don't improve the quality of the students in our city school system, we're in serious trouble."

Getting Whitmore and other leaders to recognize the problem wasn't easy. Yet for school Superintendent Peter McWalters, a key player in the Rochester experiment, it was a prerequisite to any serious talk about a new teachers contract, which he considered the centerpiece for reform. McWalters knew that before he and his school board and the union could tackle any education issue, the right people had to be brought on board—the business and community leaders who could provide financial and political support for a long-term commitment. And that is where Bill Johnson could help.

Bacon, eggs and facts

As head of the local Urban League and father of three children, Johnson had pointed an angry finger at the school system
for years. In 1985, after learning that barely 3 percent of the
blacks who graduated from city schools had a B average, he challenged the community to act. At his urging, a group of local leaders began meeting for breakfast, first at the home of U. of R.'s
O'Brien and later in the executive dining room in the Kodak
Tower.

McWalters brought to the bacon-and-eggs sessions a note-
book full of grim statistics that hold true today. Most prominent
among them is a dropout rate of 30 percent, which means that
nearly 1,800 students currently in the city's high schools will never graduate. One of every 5 students is suspended for poor discipline. Among those who stay, half of the seventh, eighth and
ninth graders fail at least one core subject—English, math, social
studies or science. Even in kindergarten, 4 of 5 pupils are at least
a year behind in readiness skills. "Our clients changed but we
didn't," McWalters told the executives. "We've never done well
with kids who don't conform to conventional expectations, kids
who don't act like students."

But McWalters knew that statistics alone wouldn't convince
the business leaders. He needed to bring his world to their world.
And this son of an unskilled laborer, who grew up in a tenement,
didn't mince words. "Those of you who think all that's needed is
for us to simply do the old things better are missing the point,"
he told his listeners.

It's not a question of doing it harder. It's a question of doing
it differently."

It was last spring—16 months later—when McWalters finally
realized that his message was getting through. "I could sense
twinkles going off. One person said, 'You're talking about organizational development and research and development.' Another
one turned to me and said, 'You're not talking about a two or
three-year deal, are you? This is going to take five to 10 years.'"
That, says McWalters, "was the watershed. They understood."

No one embraced the message with more vigor than Kodak's
Whitmore, whose company was in the midst of an overhaul that
included a cut of nearly 10,000 in its Rochester work force. In education, Kodak had given a helping hand mostly to colleges.

Soon, Whitmore led the company in a new direction—the city's public schools. "The best way to enhance quality is to get it right the first time," he says. "It's done in our business, and it can be done in the schools. Remediation is not the answer." Business, he says, must wed education to jobs. "For too long, we've broken the link between what kids learn and what they do with it."

That's changing. The breakfast sessions fostered a business-industry task force, which designated five executives to spend a school year studying Rochester's school district and others around the nation to find ways for business to help. From that study came the Rochester Brainpower Program, which includes an ad campaign, partnerships between businesses and schools and the placement of a company-paid job counselor in every high school.

Educating the teachers

The breakfast meetings also helped push the U. of R. out of its ivory tower. Like many big-city colleges, it historically had shown scant interest in its city schools, even while it lamented the shortcomings of their graduates. One goal when O'Brien became president four years ago was to change the university's reputation for being aloof. The schools initiative gave him an ideal opportunity. Now, the U. of R. has introduced joint faculty appointments between the Graduate School of Education and other departments in the belief that teachers don't teach education, they teach subjects. The new emphasis is not so much on "teacher education" as on the "education of teachers." City schools and the U. of R. are bringing six city teachers to the campus a few days each week as adjunct professors in the education school. The goal is for city schools to become teaching centers, as hospitals are for the university's medical school.

Much of McWalters's progress results from his credibility. He's a straight talker who lets others quote John Dewey and Horance Mann. "Student performance is the only means of evaluation I will accept," he says. "And not just for some students. All students. I no longer believe there is such a thing as a good teacher if the kids aren't learning." A Peace Corps volunteer who came to Rochester in 1970, McWalters worked mostly as a teacher until 1981 when then Superintendent Laval Wilson plucked him from the ranks and put him in charge of the districts's budget. He got the top job in 1986 after Wilson left to run Boston's schools. Un-like most of his teachers and administrators, McWalters lives in Rochester and can walk to his office. His wife Alice teaches at Monroe High, and their three daughters attend public schools.

McWalters's commitment was a factor when he began discuss-ing a new contract with Adam Urbanski, president of the Roches-ter Teachers Association. Urbanski agreed that fundamental change was needed, but he knew it would be hard to convince his 2,300 union teachers. Yet Urbanski was accustomed to chal-lenges: He fled Poland as a boy, worked his way through the Rochester school system and earned a Ph.D. from the U. of R. And the Solidarity poster in his union office served as a reminder that one man can make a difference.

As a starting point in their discussions, McWalters and Urban-ski focused on Carnegie's report on teaching. But the report failed to deal with McWalters's chief concern: Better student per-formance. "Why should I improve the lot of teachers if you can't guarantee me better results?" he asked Urbanski. To McWalters, that meant holding teachers accountable for student achieve-ment, a notion alien to most union leaders. The superintendent wanted teachers to become more closely involved in students' lives. Meanwhile, he would gain more control over the assign-ment of teachers to remedy the old problem of inexperienced teachers facing the toughest students. The plan included the right to dismiss weak teachers if peer mentoring and other inter-vention didn't work.

"The soul of the experiment"

It was a tall order for any union head, but Urbanksi didn't flinch, in part because he saw a chance to trade for things his teachers wanted. Chief among them were more money, a profes-sional career path and a real role in deciding what and how to teach.

Negotiations between the two men went on for several months at several sites, including the restaurant below Urbanski's office. Finally, after an all-night session last August, they shook hands on a contract that McWalters calls "the soul of this whole experiment." The school district agreed to raise teacher pay an average of 40 percent over three years, including a $4,500 in-crease for all teachers in the first year. Pay for first-year teachers is rising 52 percent, from $18,993 a year ago to $28,935 in 1989–90. In the third year, a veteran teacher in the new category of "lead teacher" can earn as much as $70,000. Increases in state and county aid made the pay hikes possible.

The pact also has the teachers working longer hours and extra days. In exchange, they give up the automatic pay increments for years of experience and extra education. And they agree to waive seniority rights when transferring from school to school. That means, in theory at least, that school-based planning committees, made up of teachers and administrators, will decide transfers on suitability as well as seniority. McWalters hopes this will help cull deadwood. "There are a lot of people who are just putting their time in and who want to get into a school where they can get by with less work," he says. Making teachers accountable for their work is an idea that Rochester's leaders feel is long overdue. Says David Kearns, the chairman of Xerox [and Current Undersecretary of Education]: "Teaching is the only profession I know of that, if you do well, nothing good happens to you, and if you do poorly, nothing bad happens to you."

The contract also makes universal an existing program called home-base guidance, in which one teacher becomes the mentor for a group of 20 students. McWalters calls the program, which is working well in a few schools, "a keen sense of the obvious." He adds, "I never want to hear of a kid who is doing well and then gradually starts falling through the cracks and nobody knows it." But, five months into the new contract, he admits that "there's been no revolution in attitudes. An awful lot of buck passing is still going on."

No more peanuts

Problems aside, there's evidence that the contract is making a difference. Teacher applications are up substantially. Some teachers who left the district are coming back for more money and the chance to be a part of the experiment.

Conversations in teacher lounges reflect a boost in morale. "It's nice to know you're respected," says Ed Hathaway, a computer-science teacher who started 14 years ago at below $10,000. The contract also means a change in attitude. "It used to be real easy for someone to say, 'I'm paid peanuts so why should I stay after school?'" notes Len Ortenzi, 29, a fourth-year physics teach-

er at Wilson Magnet High. "That's not as easy to say any more."
With the $4,500 raise, Ortenzi now makes $26,500 a year—
hardly a gold mine for a man with a wife and a 3-year-old daugh-
ter—but it means he won't leave the profession.

The new contract hasn't pleased all of Ortenzi's colleagues.
Nearly 170 teachers voted against the pact. "It spells out a mar-
velous vision of the teacher's role," says James Grattan, who has
taught English for 17 years, "but it leaves too many of the specif-
ics to be worked out." Teachers worry, too, that they will be
judged solely by whether student test scores improve. Whatever
the measure, says the school board's Curry, "the pressure is now
on the teachers. They certainly can't say they're underpaid."

The first five months of the contract prove that the age-old
rivalry between teachers and administrators is still very much
alive. Administrators fret that lines of authority and accountability will become blurred. And many teachers still see administrators back at district headquarters as meddling bureaucrats. A key
component of the contract—"school-based planning"—could be
transformed from a laudable idea to a source of confusion and resentment if the mistrust, fear and incompetence among and between teachers and administrators aren't overcome.

Parents are another problem. When Bill Johnson of the Urban League attends parent-teacher conferences at his daughters'
school, he can see by the low attendance that not enough parents
are doing their part. The school district is exploring new ways to
involve parents. McWalters is urging business leaders to let workers off to visit teachers during school hours. "If an executive
needs to go to his kid's school, he goes," he says. "But his secretary
can't do that." Urbanski wants to require parents of pupils with
failing grades to come in person to pick up the report cards.

Perhaps Rochester's biggest enemy will be the patience of its
people. Expectations are high. Indeed, Urbanski already hears
complaints about too few results. "We have to convince the public
that asking for a 10-year experiment does not mean we're welch-
ing on the deal." Still, he and the others are confident they can
pull it off. "We're going to get there, but it won't happen if everyone is looking at their watches."

From a window near his third-floor classroom, Dante Hooker
can easily see the Kodak and Xerox towers and the other tall
buildings that house the banks, corporations and institutions that
represent much of Rochester's success. For many of the city's

young adults, that success is a world away, and it may always be so. But if Rochester's plan to turn around its schools succeeds, Dante and thousands of kids like him may not have to always look at that world from afar.

BIBLIOGRAPHY

An asterisk (*) preceding a reference indicates an excerpt from the work has been reprinted in their compilation.

BOOKS AND PAMPHLETS

Alatis, James and Staczek, John. Perspectives on bilingualism and bilingual education. Georgetown University Press. '85.

Ambert, Alba. Bilingual education and English as a second language. Garland. '88.

Ambert, Alba and Melendez, Sarah. Bilingual education: a sourcebook. Teachers College Press, Columbia University. '87.

Arons, Stephen. Compelling belief: the culture of American schooling. University of Massachusetts. '86.

Arora, R. K. and Duncan, C. G. Multicultural education: towards good practice. Routledge & Kegan Paul. '86.

August, Diane and Garcia, Eugene. Language minority education in the United States: research, policy, and practice. C. C. Thomas. '88.

Bacharach, Samuel B. Education reform: making sense of it all. Allyn and Bacon. '90.

Baker, Colin. Key issues in bilingualism and bilingual education. Multilingual Matters. '88.

Banks, James A. Multiethnic education: theory and practice. Allyn and Bacon. '88.

Banks, James and Banks, Cherry. Multicultural education: issues and perspectives. Allyn and Bacon. '89.

Bennett, Christine I. Comprehensive multicultural education: theory and practice. Allyn and Bacon. '90.

Berryman, Sue E. Shadows in the wings: the next educational reform. National Center on Education and Employment. '87.

Beyer, Landon and Apple, Michael W. The curriculum: problems, politics, and possibilities. State University of New York Press. '88.

Bialystok, Ellen. Language processing in bilingual children. Cambridge University Press. '91.

Bredemeier, Mary E. Urban classroom portraits: teachers who make a difference. Lang. '88.

Bullough, Robert V. The forgotten dream of American public education. Iowa State University Press. '88.

Bunzel, John H. Challenge to American schools: the case for standards and values. Oxford University Press. '85.

Bush, Tony. Directors of education: facing reform. Jessica Kingsley. '89.

Butts, R. Freeman. The civic mission in educational reform. Hoover Institution Press. '89.

Chitty, Clyde. Towards a new education system: the victory of the New Right? Falmer Press. '89.

Cohen, Sol and Solomon, Lewis. From the campus: perspectives on the school reform movement. Praeger. '89.

Craft, James. Bilingual education: history, politics, theory, and practice. Falmer Press. '84.

Crawford, James. Bilingual education: history, politics, theory, and practice. Crown Publishing Company. '89.

Cummins, Jim. Empowering minority students. California Association for Bilingual Education. '89.

Cummins, Jim and Swain, Merrill. Bilingualism in education aspects of theory, research, and practice. Longman. '86.

Derman-Sparks, Louise. Anti-bias curriculum: tools for empowering young children. National Association for the Education of Young People. '89.

DeVitis, Joseph and Sola, Andrew. Building bridges for educational reform: new approaches to teacher education. Iowa State University Press. '89.

Elmore, Richard F. Restructuring schools: the next generation of educational reform. Jossey-Bass. '90.

Elmore, Richard and McLaughlin, Milbrey. Steady work: policy, practice, and the reform of American education. Rand Corporation. '88.

Fantini, Mario D. Regaining excellence in education. Merrill. '86.

Ferguson, Henry. Manual for multicultural education. International Press. '87.

Fine, Michael. Framing dropouts: notes on the politics of an urban public high school. State University of New York Press. '90.

Foster, Peter. Policy and practice in multicultural and anti-racist education: a case study of a multi-ethnic comprehensive school. Routledge. '90.

Flude, Michael and Hammer, Merril. The Education Reform Act, 1988: its origins and implications. Falmer Press. '89.

Fradd, Sandra and Weismanthel, M. Jeanne. Meeting the needs of culturally and linguistically different students; a handbook for educators. Little Brown. '89.

Garcia, Eugene, Lomeli, Francisco, and Ortiz, Isidoro. Chicano studies: a multidisciplinary approach. Teachers College Press. '84.

Garcia, Eugene E. and Padilla, Raymond V. Advance in bilingual education research. University of Arizona Press. '85.

Gay, Kathlyn. Crisis in education: will the United States be ready for the year 2000? F. Watts. '86.

Genesee, Fred. Learning through two languages: studies in immersion and bilingual education. Newbury House. '87.

Gillborn, David. Race, ethnicity, and education: teaching and learning in multi ethnic schools. Unwin Hyman. '90.

Gollnick, Donna and Chinn, Philip. Multicultural education in a pluralistic society. Merrill. '90.

Gonzalez, Gilbert G. Chicano education in the era of segregation. Balah Institute Press. '90.

Gross, Beatrice and Gross, Ronald. The great school debate: which way for American education? Simon & Schuster. '85.

Grugeon, Elizabeth and Woods, Peter. Educating all: multicultural perspectives in the primary school. Routledge. '90.

Guthrie, Grace Pung. A school divided: an ethnography of bilingual education in a Chinese community. L. Erlbaum. '85.

Hargreaves, Andy. Curriculum and assessment reform. Open University Press. '89.

Hessari, Ruth and Hill, Dave. Practical ideas for multicultural learning and teaching in the primary classroom. Routledge. '89.

Hosch, Harmon M. Attitudes toward bilingual education: a view from the border. Texas Western Press. '84.

Hulmes, Edward. Education and cultural diversity. Longman. '89.

Imhoff, Gary. Learning in two languages: from conflict to consensus. Transatlantic Publishers. '90.

Isser, Natalie and Schwartz, Lita. The American school and the melting pot: minority self-esteem and public education. Wyndham Hall Press. '85.

Jacobson, Stephen and Conway, James. Educational leadership in an age of reform. Longman. '90.

Kagan, Sharon Lynn and Zigler, Edward. Early schooling: the national debate. Yale University Press. '87.

Katz, Michael B. Reconstructing American education. Harvard University Press. '87.

Lemlech, Johanna. Handbook for successful urban teaching. University Press of America. '84.

Lessow-Hurley, Judith. The foundation of dual language instruction. Longman. '90.

Levine, Josie and Bleach, Jean. Bilingual learners in the mainstream curriculum. Falmer Press. '90.

Lightfoot, Alfred. Urban education in social perspective. University Press of America. '85.

Louis, Karen and Miles, Matthew. Improving the urban high school: what works and why. Teachers College Press. '90.

Lynch, James. Multicultural education: principles and practice. Routledge & Kegan Paul. '86.

Macchiarola, Frank and Hauser, Thomas. For our children: a different approach to public education. Continuum. '85.

Margolis, Edwin and Moses, Stanley. An elusive quest: the struggle for equality of educational opportunity. Associated Faculty Press. '88.

Modgil, Sohan. Multicultural education: the interminable debate. Falmer Press. '86.

Nash, Ronald H. The closing of the American heart: what's really wrong with America's schools. Probe Books. '90.

National Commission on Secondary Schooling for Hispanics. Make something happen: Hispanics and urban high school reform. Hispanic Policy Development Project. '84.

Nixon, Jon. A teacher's guide to multicultural education. Blackwell. '85.

Ovando, Carolos and Collier, Virginia. Bilingual and ESL classrooms: teaching in multicultural contexts. McGraw-Hill. '85.

Padillo, Amado, Fairchild, Halford, Concepcion, Valadez. Bilingual education: issues and strategies. Sage. '90.

Payne, Charles M. Getting what we ask for: the ambiguity of success and failure in urban education. University Press of America. '84.

Porter, Rosalie. Forked tongue: the politics of bilingual education. Basic Books. '90.

Pumfrey, Peter and Verma, Gajendra. Race relations and urban education: contexts, and promising practices. Falmer Press. '90.

Ramirez, Arnulfo. Bilingualism through schooling: cross cultural education for minority and majority students. State University of New York Press. '85.

Ramsey, Patricia G. Teaching and learning in a diverse world: multicultural education for young children. Teachers College. Columbia University. '87.

Ramsey, Patricia, Vold, Edwina, and Williams, Leslie. Multicultural education: a source book. Garland. '89.

Reyhmer, Jon A. Teaching the Indian child: a bilingual/multicultural approach. Eastern Montana College. '86.

Robinson, Gail. Crosscultural understanding: processes and approaches for foreign language, English as a second language, and bilingual educators. Pergamon. '85.

Sarason, Seymour B. The predictable failure of educational reform: can we change course before it's too late? Jossey-Bass. '90.

Schlechty, Phillip C. Schools for the twenty-first century: leadership imperatives for educational reform. Jossey-Bass. '90.

Shea, Christine, Kahane, Ernest, and Sola, Peter. The new servants of power: a critique of the 1980s school reform movement. Greenwood. '89.

Sikkema, Mildred and Niyekawa, Agnes. Design for cross-cultural learning. Intercultural Press. '87.

Sleeter, Christine E. and Grant, Carl. Making choices for multicultural education: five approaches to race, class, and gender. Merrill. '88.

Stein, Colman. Sink or swim: the politics of bilingual education. Praeger. '86.

Stewart, Alva. Education reform in the United States: a bibliographic survey. Van Bibliographies. '88.

*Task Force on Minorities: Equity and Excellence. A Curriculum of Inclusion. New York State Education Department. '89.

Tiedt, Pamela and Tiedt, Iris. Multicultural teaching: a handbook of activities, information, and resources. Allyn and Bacon. '90.

Tomlinson, Tommy M. and Walberg, Herbert J. Academic work and educational excellence: raising student productivity. McCutchan. '86.

Troyna, Barry and Carrington, Bruce. Education, racism, and reform. Routledge. '90.

Verma, Gajendra. Education for all: a land mark in pluralism. Falmer Press. '89.

Walker, J. C. and Hunt, Christine. Louts and legend: male youth culture in an inner city school. Allen & Unwin. '87.

Williams, James and Snipper, Grace. Literacy and bilingualism. Longman. '90.

Williams, Michael R. Neighborhood organizing for urban school reform. Teachers College Press. '89.

Williams, Leslie and De Gaetano, Yvonne. A multicultural bilingual approach to teaching young children. Addison-Wesley. '85.

Willie, Charles and Miller, Inabeth. Social goals and educational reform: American schools in the twentieth century. Greenwood. '88.

Wurzel, Jaime. Toward multiculturalism: a reader in multicultural education. Intercultural Press. '88.

ADDITIONAL PERIODICAL ARTICLES WITH ABSTRACTS

For those who wish to read more widely on the subject of the state of American education, this section contains abstracts of additional articles that bear on the topic. Readers who require a comprehensive list of materials are advised to consult the *Reader's*

Guide to Periodical Literature and other Wilson indexes.

Enroute with an education president: notes and quotes. John W. Donohue. *America* 162:342-4+ Ap 7 '90

President Bush has proclaimed that U. S. students will be first in the world in math and science by the year 2000, but there is not enough time, money, or national determination to achieve this goal. Tests have ranked U. S. high school seniors at the botton of a list of 24 industrialized nations in terms of science performance. U. S. students also perform poorly in history, literature, economics, and knowledge of public affairs. Professional educators and Democrats argue that restructuring the educational system will cost large sums of money, but the Bush administration has proposed only a 2 percent increase in the education budget, and states are unlikely to raise taxes for education in the current economic climate. Hundreds of schemes for piecemeal reform have been proposed, but significant progress is unlikely until Americans decide that it is needed.

Business is becoming a substitute teacher. Elizabeth Ehrlich. *Business Week* 134-5 S 19 '88

Part of a cover story on the need for skilled labor in the United States. Corporate America, which has become passionate about school reform, is providing the resources, energy, and influence to help improve education. The effectiveness of these programs remains in doubt, however. In the Boston school system, for example, industries offered summer and permanent jobs for students in exchange for school improvement, but the dropout rate has remained at 46 percent. Many join-a-school partnerships have been created across the country, with corporate sponsors providing volunteers and donating funds and equipment for a chosen school. Some teachers oppose business aid because they fear that there will be strings attached to it. The most appropriate role for business in education may be the provision of work experience and opportunities for disadvantaged youths.

The education crisis: what business can do. Nancy J. Perry. *Fortune* 118:70-3+ Jl 4 '88

A special report discussed business's increasingly active role in public school reform. Businesses are finally taking a comprehensive role in helping to overhaul the educational system. Their efforts are focusing on secondary, primary and preschool education. On the national level, businesses can provide the direction and leadership necessary for reform; on the state level, they can promote new legislation; and on the local level, they can let schools know precisely what skills they will be looking for prospective in employees. Business leaders' efforts in education are motivated by their realization that over the next 15 years, the decreasing labor pool of young people will force industry to hire traditionally less skilled and underutilized population groups.

Saving our schools. *Fortune 121 Special Issue*: 8-10+ Spr '90

A special issue on education examines how business leaders are helping in the effort to improve education. In the battle to improve American education, progress against illiteracy, innumeracy, and indifference has been slow. Despite more than 300 studies and increases in teachers' salaries and per-pupil spending, student achievement hasn't improved at all in the last seven years. Business leaders, however, are at the forefront of the drive to turn the situation around. This involvement has led to criticism regarding possible ulterior motives, but businesses have good reason to want to get involved: the improvement of America's global competitiveness. Articles explore the roles parents corporations, computers, executives, and government are and should be taking in American education.

Shortest education presidency? *National Review* 41:11-12 Mr 24 '89

George Bush has made a serious blunder in selecting Lauro F. Cavazos as secretary of education. The appointment of Cavazos, who comes from the education establishment, has delighted education associations, lobbyists, and unionists. Instead of criticizing higher education's rootless curricula, politicized faculties, wasteful institutions, and exorbitant prices, Cavazos has expressed dismay that the Office of Management and Budget hasn't found more funds for higher education. He appears to have no strategy for dealing with the nation's decrepit primary and secondary schools, other than commenting that youngsters are dropping out.

Not just for nerds. *Newsweek* 115:52-7+ Ap 9 '90

A special section examines the crisis in U. S. science education. The continued poor performance of U. S. students in international comparisons of scientific competence has led to the conclusion that Americans are in dire need of more and better technical education. Most experts agree that American science education does nothing to nurture children's natural curiosity toward the sciences. If more students do not become interested in scientific careers, they fear, there will be a shortage of Ph.D. scientists by the mid 1990s. In addition, the need for critical perspective on scientific findings is paramount. School boards, corporations, foundations, and the federal government have launched ambitious initiatives, such as the revision of school curricula, the provision of funding, and the training of teachers, to help create a more science-savvy populace. Articles examine attempted remedies, test the reader's scientific vocabulary, and profile three science educators.

Foreign policies. John Cummings. *Omni* (New York, N. Y.) 12:99-100 Ap '90

Part of a special section on education. The American educational system is failing, while systems in countries like Japan, China, and West Germany are excelling. The United States is looking to these countries for ideas on how to improve, but adapting a new system is difficult because of unique multiethnic social mores and cultural values that exist in the United States. Several foreign educational systems are described.

Bad news about math. Ezra Bowen. *Time* 129:65 Ja 26 '87

Three new studies rank American students in grades 1 through 12 low in mathematical skills in comparison with those of other countries. The studies, which were carried out by University of Michigan psychologist Harold Stevenson and University of Illinois Education professor Kenneth Travers, were the focus of a symposium convened in Washington last week by the National Research Council. In one text, the average scores of Chicago school students were found to be far below those of students in three cities in China and Japan. Another revealed the comparatively small percentage of American college-bound students who take calculus and the poor command of geometry among U. S. middle schoolers. Suggested causes for the poor showing include a lack of emphasis on math in the United States and the failure of the country's spiraling system of education. Travers is convinced that the United States must upgrade the quality of its math education if it is to survive as a high-tech society.

How to tackle school reform. Susan Tifft. *Time* 134:46-7 Ag 14 '89

Three states have enacted school reform programs that can serve as models for other parts of the country. Six years ago, the federally sponsored report A Nation at Risk warned that the quality of education in U. S. public schools was declining. Since then, as many as 16 states have restructured their school systems and increased spending on education. Arkansas has lengthened the school day and instituted a competency exam for teachers. South Carolina's Educational Improvement Act of 1984 calls for mandatory kindergarten for 5 year olds and exit exams for high school graduates. West Virginia recently approved a $1.2 billion package that provides for higher teacher salaries, teacher pensions, school construction, and basic-skills and advanced-placement programs. These programs have helped raise test scores and reduce dropout rates. The key to success for all of these states has been cooperation between state officials, business leaders, educators, and parents.

CURRICULUM

Bilingual miseducation. Abigail M. Thernstrom. *Commentary* 89:44-8 F '90

Bilingual education, in its current form, often hurts rather than helps children who have limited proficiencies in English. Ever since the adoption of the Bilingual Education Act in 1968, bilingual instruction has been presented less as an educational issue than as a political one. Its apparent aims are to ease immigrant children's transition to English-language education and to strengthen their self esteem by honoring their native languages and cultural heritages. Too often, however, educators subordinate the first goal to the second in the belief that an ethnocentric

society must mend its ways. Children are never really taught English, and
they are encouraged to think of themselves as permanently separate from
American culture. As a result, they complete their schooling without
learning the basic skills that they need to thrive in the United States.

Do we want Quebec here?. Howard Banks. *Forbes* 145:62+ Je 11
'90

Bilingualism undermines the assimilation of diverse nationalities into a
new nationality, the basis on which the United States has been built. Bilingual teaching began as an approach to teaching English to children with
limited English proficiency. Because the largest number of immigrants today come from Spanish-speaking countries, Spanish now dominates the
federally funded bilingual education program. One indication of the bilingual program's failure is the high dropout rate of Hispanic high school
students, roughly double that of blacks and whites. The groups that most
benefit from these programs are Hispanic politicians, bureaucrats whose
careers depend on the programs, and the providers of textbooks in Spanish. A constitutional amendment to make English the official U. S. language, proposed by former senator S. I. Hayakawa, might solve the
problem.

A call for disunity. Michael Novak. *Forbes* 146:65 Jl 9 '90

Attempts to downplay the European influence on U. S. culture and institutions could undermine the principles on which the United States was
founded. For years, the United States has brought diverse people together and taught them to respect each other. This pluralistic system has been
a model for the world. Last July, however, the New York State commissioner of education issued a report calling European culture and its deriv-
atives oppressive and advocating an appreciation of the history,
achievements, aspirations, and concerns of all cultures. In reality, European cultural roots lie behind the U.S. Constitution, and European habits
and institutions have given it relevance and force. Without European-
American ideas, the United States could descend into the racial and ethnic strife that plagues the rest of the globe. For this reason, students must
continue to be taught the history behind the formation of the American
system.

The primal scene of education. Eric Donald Hirsch. *The New
York Review of Books* 36:29-35 Mr 2 '89

A standard sequence of core knowledge must be established in the elementary school curriculum for educational reform in the United States
to be truly effective. The lack of shared background knowledge has become acute in today's classrooms and is a chief cause of American students' poor showing in international educational comparisons. Students
in countries like Sweden and Canada perform much better than Americans in national scholastic tests because their educational systems have
stressed the importance of acquiring shared knowledge at an early age.
Specialists in American education argue that a standardized elementary
curriculum would produce a society of automatons, but Swedes and Cana-

dians are some of the most diverse, free-thinking people in the world. American elementary schooling, on the other hand, produces educational haves and have nots and undermines cultural literacy.

Multiculturalism can be taught only by multicultural people. Stephen Trachtenberg. *Phi Delta Kappan* 71:610-11 Ap '90

The debate over the cultural curriculum in American schools is confused. The meaning of the word culture, the extent to which Western culture is linked to other cultures, and the importance of multiculturalism to the nation's survival must be understood before any decisions on curricula can be made. Black and Hispanic students need to know that their backgrounds are just as cultural as those of Americans whose forebears came from Northern Europe, Asia, and the Middle East.

Diversity or death. June Jordan. *The Progressive* 54:16-17 Je '90

Power should be redistributed in the United States so that minorities are equally protected under the law and duly represented in government and academia. Demographic projections show that the nation's white population is shrinking and that the general population is becoming more racially, ethnically, and linguistically diverse. Power is held by only a small minority, however, and the public school system is failing the impending nonwhite majority. If the United States hopes to cohere as a union of disparate citizens, education reform should include greater emphasis on learning about foreign cultures.

Education: doing bad and feeling good. Charles Krauthammer. *Time* 135:78 F 5 '90

To exclude Eurocentrism from public school curricula in order to boost students' self esteem would be fruitless and misleading. A recent report issued by New York State's Task Force on Minorities charges that Eurocentrism in schools damages the psyches of minority youth. The task force suggests that curricular materials be prepared on the basis of multicultured contributions to the development of all aspects of our society. This would require the invention of multicultural contributions to American history, however, as American history has never been evenly multicultural. The task force's suggestion is ideology dressed up as education and aspiring to psychotherapy. Blaming the problems of today's minority youth on Eurocentrism diverts attention from the real problems that exist.

RESTRUCTURING THE SCHOOLS

Private choices for public schools. John Hood. *Conservative Digest* 15:70-3 My/Je '89

Public school systems around the country are beginning to give parents a choice of schools for their children, thus improving the quality of education and increasing diversity. In systems where choice is the rule each school must select a theme or mission that will interest students and parents. This promises to be a vast improvement over the approach of the past 20 years, in which schools have avoided conflicts over what values and viewpoints should be taught by avoiding the teaching of values altogether or by teaching a hodgepodge of values that satisfies no one. Decentralization, or the turning over of school control to local boards of parents and school personnel, is one popular reform regarded as a step toward full-choice systems, as are magnet schools within systems. Only when private and parochial schools are included through voucher plans, however, will both rich and poor families have the truly free choice that would lead to the best education for all.

Education reform as a conservative fiasco. Myron Lieberman. *The Education Digest* 65:3-5 Mr '90

An article condensed from the November/December 1989 Cato Policy Report examines the shortcomings of the conservative view on education reform. Conservatives have failed to enact changes that would improve public education because they have failed to understand what has to be done and why. By understating the cost of public education, conservatives weaken the case for the various forms of privatization and competition that would result in significant reforms. Further, conservatives have enthusiastically supported public school choice as a reform measure, but they do not understand that effective competition does not exist in the public school market. Competition is needed to improve education, but it will only be meaningful if it entails greater involvement by for-profit schools.

American perestroika?. Peter Brimelow. *Forbes* 145:82-6 My 14 '90

Despite all the talk of reform in recent years, American education has shown little sign of improvement. The educational system bears uncomfortable similarities to institutions that function under socialism. Basically owned and run by the government, it suffers from politicized allocation of resources, a top-heavy bureaucracy. chronic mismatching of supply and demand, and reliance on top-down panaceas to effect change. Rhetoric, reform, and more money have only engendered lower educational productivity. The solution may be to give American education a dose of capitalism by returning schools to the private sector. Parents could be aided in paying for their children's education in such a privatized system by increasing the income tax deduction for each child or by taking the money currently spent on public schools and giving it to parents in the form of vouchers. Tables and graphs depict the failure of increased spending and other efforts at reform in the 1980s.

The blackboard jungle revisited. Geoffrey Morris. *National Review* 41:18-19 My 5 '89

The problems of inner-city schools are in the national spotlight. The state of New Jersey took control of the Jersey City school district because the school board could not deal with the district's high dropout rate, low test scores, drugs, and violence. Joe Clark, a high school principal in Paterson, New Jersey has become famous for his disciplinary style that attempted to reverse the no-hope ghetto mentality of his students. Students need a moral framework to interpret life's lessons but state-supported schools shy away from values education, which smacks of religion. A fundamental reform, such as a voucher system that would allow low-income families to choose between private, parochial, and public schools, would take the government out of the picture, allowing the integration of moral education into daily lessons.

The public school lobby vs. educational vouchers. Dwight R. Lee, Robert L. Sexton. *USA Today* (Periodical) 117:79-81 S '88

Vouchers that put money in the hands of education consumers would foster competition and ultimately reform the public education system. Consumers currently pay taxes whether they use the public school system or not, and students are in effect captive clients. Educators take advantage of this situation and pay less attention to consumers and more to job perquisites. In a voucher or tax credit system, however, schools would have to compete for students and respond to the educational decisions of consumers. If survival were dependent on meeting consumer demands, public schools would fail, and they have resisted such changes. Private schools have opposed voucher plans because they fear a loss of autonomy due to the receipt of public funds, but no experimental system thus far has fairly addressed these or other concerns. Reforms, like vouchers, will only be possible when the facade that hides public schools' special-interest politics is weakened.

Restructuring American education through choice. Lauro Fred Cavazos. *Vital Speeches of the Day* 55:514-16 Je 15 '89

In an address delivered to the Education Press Association, the U. S. secretary of education argues that choice should be the cornerstone of the restructuring of elementary and secondary education. He notes that choice reforms would allow students and parents to determine which school would provide the best educational opportunities for them. He argues that choice would allow schools to meet the needs of some students exceptionally well instead of meeting the needs of all students minimally well. He also contends that it would empower parents to participate in educational decision making, giving teachers and principals control over their curricula, and encourage students to learn.

URBAN EDUCATION

Urban teachers: their new colleagues and curriculum. Carl A. Grant. *Phi Delta Kappan* 70:764-70 Je '89

The most urgent tasks facing urban teachers are the socialization of their new, often unprepared colleagues and the development of a curriculum that addresses the needs of urban students. Teacher training typically includes little information on the multicultural world of urban students, leaving new teachers vulnerable to culture shock. The racial, sexual, and economic preconceptions of new teachers about minorities can also limit their effectiveness. Meanwhile, the new curricular emphasis on predetermined and quantifiable skills ignores urban students' interests and goals. School studies should not marginalize students' lives outside the classroom.

Reconstructing the nation's worst schools. Herbert J. Walberg, Michael J. Bakalis and Joseph L. Bast. *Phi Delta Kappan* 70:802-5 Je '89

Chicagoans United to Reform Education (CURE) has instituted plans at legislative and community levels to amend the Chicago school system. Known as the nation's worst, Chicago public schools have had dropout rates as high as 75 percent and test scores well below the national average, in spite of spending more per pupil than 31 of the 50 largest school systems in the nation. CURE is decentralizing the schools' power structure and streamlining the massive school bureaucracy. Chicago's present school board will be disbanded, and parents, teachers, and principals can involve themselves in the most important decisions via elected school governing councils. Central office spending will be reduced by 25 percent in the first year, with the money allocated to schools. Education rebates to taxpayers making tuition payments to registered Chicago schools are also being considered.

A blueprint for better schools. Jerry Buckley. *U. S. News & World Report* 104:60-5 Ja 18 '88

The school district of Rochester, New York, is launching an educational experiment that could radically alter how the city's schools are operated and could become a model of reform for other school districts. Rochester's ambitious plan, entitled A Region Prepared, gives teachers and administrators in individual schools a bigger say in the decision-making process and makes them more accountable for student performance. It also targets at risk students, who make up a majority of the school population, and advocates changes in the training and hiring of teachers. The most visible sign of the changes is a new contract making Rochester's teachers among the highest paid anywhere. Some critics fear that the $31 million venture will prove too expensive and will do little to boost student achievement. Although many details remain to be worked out, national education experts maintain that the Rochester experiment is further along than any in the country.

Fixing the teaching, not the kids. Jerry Buckley. *U. S. News & World Report* 106:61-2 Mr 13 '89

Almost one-sixth of the students in Rochester, New York, are assigned to special-education classes, with those who are labeled learning disabled constituting the largest category. Rochester administrators are trying to reform the school system, and one step is to cut the rolls of special-education programs. They believe that referrals to such programs are often used to avoid determining what is wrong with the educational methods being used by teachers. For example, the number of poor minority students has increased over the years, and teachers, who frequently view culturally and economically different students as difficult, often refer them to special-education classes. The Discovery program at Rochester's Frederick Douglass Middle School is aimed at developing new methods of teaching and at helping special-education students return to regular classes. The program also keeps borderline students out of special classes altogether.

The hard lessons of school reform. Jerry Buckley. *U. S. News & World Report* 106:58-60 Je 26 '89

For the past two years, Rochester, New York, has been engaged in an ambitious effort to improve its schools that has made the city a model for urban education reform. The reforms have not yet translated into major improvements in the performance of the district's 32,000 students, but there has been progress. The core leadership that launched the experiment is growing, the business community and national education experts are participating, teachers have become more involved with their students, and some innovative programs have been created. The key figures in the experiment are superintendent of schools Peter McWalters, teachers' union leader Adam Urbanski, Eastman Kodak president Kay Whitmore, and Marc Tucker, president of the National Center on Education and the Economy.